Undergraduate Topics in Computer Science

Series editor

Ian Mackie

Undergraduate Topics in Computer Science (UTiCS) delivers high-quality instructional content for undergraduates studying in all areas of computing and information science. From core foundational and theoretical material to final-year topics and applications, UTiCS books take a fresh, concise, and modern approach and are ideal for self-study or for a one- or two-semester course. The texts are all authored by established experts in their fields, reviewed by an international advisory board, and contain numerous examples and problems. Many include fully worked solutions.

More information about this series at http://www.springer.com/series/7592

Bhim P. Upadhyaya

Data Structures
and Algorithms with Scala

A Practitioner's Approach with Emphasis
on Functional Programming

 Springer

Bhim P. Upadhyaya
EqualInformation, LLC
Sunnyvale, CA, USA

ISSN 1863-7310   ISSN 2197-1781   (electronic)
Undergraduate Topics in Computer Science
ISBN 978-3-030-12560-8   ISBN 978-3-030-12561-5   (eBook)
https://doi.org/10.1007/978-3-030-12561-5

Library of Congress Control Number: 2019930577

This Springer imprint is published by the registered company Springer Nature Switzerland AG
The registered company address is: Gewerbestrasse 11, 6330 Cham, Switzerland

To the Readers
-Bhim

Preface

Professional software engineers find it difficult to make time to upgrade and reinforce their own knowledge; most of their time is spent on business responsibilities. This is also true for engineering students (among others), who have numerous courses to take and rigorous exercises to do. So, time is a constraint for almost everybody. It is our observation that professionals need concise information source in order to be able to allocate and get value out of their time. In this context, it is handy to have a book that can be reviewed in one or two weekends.

A quick survey of books on *Data Structures and Algorithms* reveals that there are plenty of well-written books; however, they have multiple shortcomings. One that stands out is that most of those books were written a decade back. Computer science is one of the fastest - if not the fastest - changing fields. There is a saying: *every time you turn your head you might see something new*, which is true, specially with the advances in automated builds. There might be thousands of builds running or completing at a given point in time. All the successful builds create new versions of existing software packages or new software packages. In this rapidly changing context, books written a decade or more ago may not serve the purpose best.

Another shortcoming of well-written classical books in this field is that they are either too long or too theoretical for practitioners. Finding weeks of free time to read a book is certainly challenging for working software engineers, amid their stringent work responsibilities. Also, too-theoretical books might be good for intellectual exercises and research in the field, but may not serve well to solve applied problems quickly. Most professional engineers look for terse and precise presentation of material.

The third aspect is that there are not many *Data Structures and Algorithms* books available for Scala. Scala is becoming popular in the big data space. Most senior Java-based software jobs, these days, prefer Scala proficiency. In this context, it is certainly helpful to be equipped with Scala implementations of popular data structures as well as algorithms. Most of the analytical tasks are better done by the functional style of processing. As Scala is an object-functional language, we can do multi-paradigm programming. Scala also supports polyglot programming, Java being the closest sibling.

This book has been written more in a study-note or tutorial style and it covers nine popular topics in *Data Structures and Algorithms*—arrays, lists, stacks, queues, hash tables, binary trees, sorting, searching, and graphs. Arrays are implemented in an *imperative style* with the famous matrix multiplication problem. Most of the other topics are implemented in a *functional style*. So, if you are planning to learn a functional version of *Data Structures and Algorithms* in Scala, this is the right book. I've tried to make the book as accessible as possible.

Most of the programs in this book are complete and running applications. Also, each topic or subtopic has at least one complete and running example, which will save your time. You can try to come up with better implementations than in this book. Most of the challenge exercises are for this purpose. However, some are intended to reinforce your understanding of the existing material. In addition to creativity, the ability to take somebody else's solution and improve is desirable in the job market; I've tried to incorporate both in this book. Also the book includes solution to exercises so that you don't struggle, specially when you are time-bound. Happy Reading!

Sunnyvale, California   *Bhim P. Upadhyaya*
October 2018

Contents

List of Figures

List of Tables

Abbreviations

API	Application Programming Interface
AQL	Array-Oriented Query Language
AWS	Amazon Web Services
BFS	Breadth-First Search
BST	Binary Search Tree
CPU	Central Processing Unit
DFS	Depth-First Search
FIFO	First In First Out
HTML	Hyptertext Markup Language
LIFO	Last In First Out
LOC	Line Of Code
SQL	Structured Query Language
WWW	World Wide Web
XML	Extensible Markup Language

Chapter 1
Foundational Components

We have observed that the longer professional engineers work, the more they tend to focus on advanced topics and problems with higher complexity. When this is practiced for a long time, it is easy to forget the fundamental building blocks. As a result, solutions proposed for advanced problems may be biased. In order to have a balanced approach, in this chapter, we focus on basic building blocks and fundamental algorithms. Feel free to skip this chapter if you do not need a refresher on fundamentals.

We will focus more on what we can do with the fundamental structures than an exhaustive listing of APIs that can be found in online documentation, even though we might occasionally list the available features if this is helpful for memorization that leads to productivity. In software engineering job interviews, even though interviewers don't focus on memorizing APIs, they do appreciate the ability to remember available features and use them to solve problems promptly. This is desirable at work as well. So there should be a balance between creative ability and knowledge of existing tools. In many cases, such knowledge can speed up the implementation of creative ideas. We will make use of all such opportunities when we explore fundamental building blocks in this chapter.

In this book, we use Scala as our vehicle to implement data structures and algorithms. Hence, in the next section, we will cover Scala arrays. Arrays are the core building blocks of imperative programming. The majority of high-level programming languages support array structures. Different forms of arrays can also be found in low-level computational infrastructures, such as memory and CPU. We will be using arrays extensively in this book. More importantly, many other data structures use arrays directly or indirectly. We discuss arrays-based computation, in detail, in Chapter 3.

Lists are fundamental building blocks of functional programming. We are very likely to find lists in almost all the functional programming languages available today. One of the earliest high-level programming languages, *List Processor (LIST)*, focuses on list-based processing; it builds on the idea of recursive functions of symbolic expressions. Scala has brought together many features from many different programming languages, including historical functional programming languages

© Springer Nature Switzerland AG 2019
B. P. Upadhyaya, *Data Structures and Algorithms with Scala*, Undergraduate
Topics in Computer Science, https://doi.org/10.1007/978-3-030-12561-5_1

such as LISP and ML, and more recent functional languages like Haskell. Scala is also an expression-oriented language, along with being object-oriented and functional. In this context, spending some time with list fundamentals is certainly going to pay off in the long run. Section 1.2 covers list fundamentals. This section will also cover another important foundational block called *Vector*. We will see in this section why we need vectors. Detailed list-based computation is discussed in Chapter 4.

In many practical applications, continuous streams of data need to be handled. Some of the examples of such applications are Twitter feed processing, server logs processing, social media interactions like Facebook activities, etc. In these applications, very large streams of data are generated by user activities. Since user activities relate to business opportunities, many companies spend significant sums on stream processing. These days, there are numerous frameworks that support stream processing, including open source frameworks such as Apache Spark, Apache Kafka, and Apache Storm. At the time of writing, Spark and Kafka are the two latest and most important frameworks in *big data*. Both of these frameworks were mostly written in Scala. Hence we will cover Scala streams in Section 1.4. Then we will cover sliding windows in the subsequent section.

1.1 Arrays

Scala arrays are mutable collections of values and are indexed. This means we can access any element of an array if we know its index in $O(1)$ running time. Refer to Section B.3 for asymptotic notations and their meanings. Let's look at the following code snippet.

```
scala> val myNumbers = Array(0, 2, 4, 6, 8, 10)
myNumbers: Array[Int] = Array(0, 2, 4, 6, 8, 10)

scala> myNumbers(5)
res0: Int = 10
```

In the code snippet above, we define the array *myNumbers* without using the reserved word *new*. Scala allows us to write succinct code and it does the necessary internal transformations for the programmer. An array index starts from 0, so the element at position *n* is accessed using `<array-name>(n-1)`. In our case *myNumbers*(5) returns an integer at position 6, which is 10. This call is internally translated to *apply(Int)*. It is interesting to go through the GitHub source code (`https://github.com/scala/scala/blob/2.13.x/src/library/scala/Array.scala`), if you have time. Here, since we are more interested in using arrays rather than creating array structures for the purpose of implementing a programming language, we will use the API documentation and try some interesting operations that are widely used in day to day programming.

Let's look at the following code snippet now.

```
scala> val numMult2 = myNumbers.map(_ * 2)
```

```
numMult2: Array[Int] = Array(0, 4, 8, 12, 16, 20)
```

We multiply each number in the array by 2 and assign the result to *numMult2*. Now if we execute *numMult*(5), we get 20. Note how terse the code is. If we try to achieve the same using imperative loops, we will end up writing several lines of code (LOCs). Let's write one and see the difference.

```
package com.equalinformation.dascala.scala
    .fundamentals

object MultBy2App {
    def main(args: Array[String]): Unit = {
        val myNumbers = Array(0, 2, 4,6, 8, 10)
        multBy2(myNumbers).foreach(println)
    }

    def multBy2(myArray: Array[Int]): Array[Int] = {
        val size = myArray.length
        val myTempArray = new Array[Int](size)
        var i = 0
        while(i < size) {
            myTempArray(i) = myArray(i) * 2
            i += 1
        }
        myTempArray
    }
}
```

The program above has 17 LOCs, whereas our functional implementation above has a single LOC; add one more LOC for the original array definition, so a total of 2 LOCs. It is self-explanatory why functional programming is better suited for certain types of tasks. At this stage, it is important to note that length is not the only factor. There are other reason like scalability, concurrency, distribution, etc. In this chapter, we will try to be more functional than imperative.

Now, let's see some interesting array features. Reversing an array can be done by using the *reverse* operation as shown below.

```
scala> myNumbers.reverse
res0: Array[Int] = Array(10, 8, 6, 4, 2, 0)
```

Two arrays can be combined using the ++ operator as shown below.

```
scala> val array1 = Array(1,2,3,4,5)
array1: Array[Int] = Array(1, 2, 3, 4, 5)

scala> val array2 = Array(6,7,8,9,10)
array2: Array[Int] = Array(6, 7, 8, 9, 10)
```

```
scala> array1 ++ array2
res2: Array[Int] = Array(1, 2, 3, 4, 5, 6, 7, 8,
    9, 10)
```

If we do this in an imperative style, it will have numerous LOCs. You can try this as an exercise to get a feeling for the importance of the functional style of programming.

Now, let's try buit-in sorting.

```
scala> val fruits = Array("banana", "apple","orange")
fruits: Array[String] = Array(banana, apple, orange)

scala> fruits.sorted
res5: Array[String] = Array(apple, banana, orange)
```

Sorting is very handy in day-to-day programming. In the worst case, it takes $O(n)$ time to find an element in an unsorted array if we do not know the index beforehand. If it is sorted it takes $O(lg\ n)$ running time, which is significantly lower than $O(n)$.

We can check whether an element exists in an array by passing a predicate. In the following code snippet, a parameterized predicate is applied for every element in the array *fruits*. If the predicate holds true a boolean value *true* is returned. If there are duplicate elements, only one boolean value *true* is returned.

```
scala> fruits.exists(x => x == "banana")
res21: Boolean = true
```

If we want filter the elements of an array that satisfy a given predicate then we can do that using a *filter* operation. If there are duplicate elements, all will be listed.

```
scala> val myNums = Array(1, 2, 2, 3, 4, 5, 6, 7, 7,
    8, 9, 5, 9, 10)
myNums: Array[Int] = Array(1, 2, 2, 3, 4, 5, 6, 7,
    7, 8, 9, 5, 9, 10)

scala> myNums.filter(x => x == 2)
res33: Array[Int] = Array(2, 2)
```

Now, let's find all the even numbers in the array *myNums*. For this, we filter the array elements whose remainder is zero when divided by 2.

```
scala> myNums.filter(x => x % 2 == 0)
res35: Array[Int] = Array(2, 2, 4, 6, 8, 10)
```

Finding elements in a container is a common need for programmers. This can be achieved using the *find* operation on a given array. Next, let's see how the *find* operation works. In the result below, we see only one 2. The *find* operation returns an *Option*, and in the event of multiple occurrences, it returns the first occurrence. Since it returns an *Option*, we need to use the *get* operation on that option to get the value.

```scala
scala> myNums.find(x => x % 2 == 0)
res36: Option[Int] = Some(2)

scala> res36.get
res38: Int = 2
```

Now, let's create one more array with different data so that we can try various other operations. We pretend that the counts and the corresponding domains, subdomains, or related items are available as a single string. This is a realistic assumption because many log files store textual information, which could be treated as one very large string. In our case, we have numerous smaller strings with mixed data.

```scala
scala> val counts = Array("900,google.com",
  "60,mail.yahoo.com",
  "10,mobile.sports.yahoo.com",
  "40,sports.yahoo.com",
  "10,stackoverflow.com",
  "2,en.wikipedia.org",
  "1,es.wikipedia.org",
  "1,mobile.sports")
counts: Array[String] = Array(900,google.com,
  60,mail.yahoo.com, 10,mobile.sports.yahoo.com,
  40,sports.yahoo.com, 10,stackoverflow.com,
  2,en.wikipedia.org, 1,es.wikipedia.org,
  1,mobile.sports)
```

Next, we split the strings in such a way that the count is separated from rest of the string. This allows us to process counts.

```scala
scala> val countsMap = counts.map(_.split(",")).map {
  case Array(s1,s2) => (s1,s2) }
countsMap: Array[(String, String)] = Array(
  (900,google.com),
  (60,mail.yahoo.com),
  (10,mobile.sports.yahoo.com),
  (40,sports.yahoo.com),
  (10,stackoverflow.com),
  (2,en.wikipedia.org),
  (1,es.wikipedia.org),
  (1,mobile.sports))
```

Next, let's find the count for ".com":

```scala
scala> val comCounts = countsMap.map {
  |   case(x,y) if y.endsWith(".com") => x.toInt
  |   case _ => 0
  | }.reduceLeft(_ + _)
comCounts: Int = 1020
```

Including subdomains, the total count for ".com" domains is 1020.

Exercise 1.1. *Internet Advertisement Hits Analysis*

You are in charge of an advertising program. Your advertisements are displayed on websites all over the Internet. You have some CSV input data that counts how many times you showed an advertisement on each individual domain. Every line consists of a count and a domain name. The data looks like *counts*, above. Write a function that takes this input as a parameter and returns a data structure containing the number of hits that were recorded on each domain and each domain under it. For example, an impression on *mail.yahoo.com* counts for *mail.yahoo.com*, *yahoo.com*, and *com*. Sub domains are added to the left of their parent domains. So *mobile.sports.yahoo* and *mail* are not valid domains. A sample output is shown in Table 1.1 (note that the counts may not be correct in the sample output, these are only for illustration).

Table 1.1: Sample Internet advertisement analysis result

1220	com
800	google.com
505	yahoo.com
70	mail.yahoo.com
15	mobile.sports.yahoo.com
40	sports.yahoo.com
5	stackoverflow.com
3	org
3	wikipedia.org
2	en.wikipedia.org
1	es.wikipedia.org

1.2 Lists and Vectors

Lists are widely used in functional as well as imperative programming. As stated earlier in this chapter, some of the early high-level programming languages featured lists heavily as a part of their programming constructs. Also lists are a natural way of thinking and translating those thoughts into computational structures. If list structures are available in a programming language then programmers will use them, as there is a direct mapping between real-world lists and computational lists. We discuss list-based computation in detail in Chapter 4.

Let's first declare a list of words:

```
scala> val myFruits = List("grape", "banana",
  "apple", "mango")
myFruits: List[String] = List(grape, banana, apple,
  mango)
```

If we are dealing with the first element of a linked list for delete or update operations, this requires $O(1)$ time. Also inserting at the beginning of the list is constant time. In the *myFruits* list, if we need to locate *mango* then we need to traverse all the elements. This means that inserting an element at the end of the list also requires $O(n)$ running time. Similarly, deletion has the same time complexity for a linked list. For a very large set of data this time complexity may prove to be inefficient. In such cases, we can use another data structure called *Vector*, which has better performance; it doesn't matter whether we are performing operations in the beginning, middle, or end. *Vector* provides a similar structure to that of an array, but is immutable. We can perform many of the same operations that we can perform in lists and arrays. Internally *Vector* is implemented using *Trie* structures, which give us better performance. Many operations in *Vector* are localized and hence give constant time, $O(1)$, performance.

Let's look at a few *Vector* operation to get a feeling for vectors.

```
scala> val myFruits = Vector("grape", "banana",
  "apple", "mango")
myFruits: scala.collection.immutable.Vector[String]
  = Vector(grape, banana, apple, mango)

scala> myFruits(3)
res2: String = mango

scala> val yourFruits = Vector("cucumber", "tomato")
yourFruits: scala.collection.immutable.Vector[String]
  = Vector(cucumber, tomato)

scala> val combinedFruits = myFruits ++ yourFruits
combinedFruits: scala.collection.immutable.
  Vector[String] = Vector(grape, banana, apple,
  mango, cucumber, tomato)

scala> val notQuiteFruits = combinedFruits.filter(
  x => x == "tomato")
notQuiteFruits: scala.collection.immutable
  .Vector[String] = Vector(tomato)
```

We see that many higher level data manipulation operations are available. When we filter for a particular element, it doesn't have to traverse all the elements of the vector, *notQuiteFruits* in our case. The data are stored in a *Trie* structure, which maintains pointers to the data in a tree structure; hence the better performance.

Now let's look at one interesting and handy operation called *groupBy*, available in *List*, *Vector*, and *Array*.

```
scala> val myWords = List("dog", "cat", "rat",
  "goat", "horse")
myWords: List[String] = List(dog, cat, rat, goat,
  horse)

scala> myWords groupBy {x => x.length}
res28: scala.collection.immutable.Map[Int,
  List[String]] = Map(5 -> List(horse), 4 ->
  List(goat), 3 -> List(dog, cat, rat))
```

This partitions the traversable collection into a map of traversable collections based on a function supplied. Interestingly, if we are applying this to *List*, it produces a map containing sublists; if we are applying this to either *Array* or *Vector* it produces a map containing subarrays or sublists, respectively. In the code snippet above, it solves the problem of counting words by length.

1.3 Applied Techniques for Efficient Computation

In this section, we discuss a couple of techniques that are commonly used in the industry for better performance. Lazy evaluation, as the name suggests, allows evaluation of programming constructs when they are actually used, thereby eliminating the need for additional storage. Memoization, on the other hand, saves processing resources like CPU by storing reusable results from earlier computations.

1.3.1 Lazy Evaluation

A lazy evaluation can be defined as a kind of delayed evaluation. In this method, the evaluation of an expression is done when the value of that expression is actually used. As opposed to that, in the case of eager evaluation, expressions are evaluated at the time of program execution. Let's take a few examples.

```
scala> val myNum = 10
myNum: Int = 10

scala> var myNextNum = 11
myNextNum: Int = 11
```

In the above code snippet, both *myNum* and *myNextNum* are evaluated immediately, irrespective of whether they are used or not. Contrary to that, in the following code snippet, *lazyTime* is defined before *eagerTime* and also printed before *eagerTime*, but has higher value. This means *lazyTime* was not evaluated when the expression was executed. Note that *lazy* is a Scala reserved word.

```
scala> import java.util.Calendar
import java.util.Calendar

scala> lazy val lazyTime = Calendar.getInstance
    .getTime
lazyTime: java.util.Date = <lazy>

scala> val eagerTime = Calendar.getInstance.getTime
eagerTime: java.util.Date = Thu Nov 08 19:41:44 PST
    2018

scala> println(lazyTime)
Thu Nov 08 19:42:19 PST 2018

scala> println(eagerTime)
Thu Nov 08 19:41:44 PST 2018
```

Now, the main question is what do we gain by making evaluations lazy? In the code snippet above, we have smaller values to hold in the memory. But imagine thousands of records being evaluated. If we are not using those records then holding them in the computer's memory is wasteful. In the case of even larger data, the computation can become infeasible. Currently most popular open source big data processing engines, like Apache Spark, use lazy evaluation extensively.

Another way of making evaluation lazy is to ask the compiler for delayed parameter evaluation. This can be achieved by using functions as parameters. Let's take a look at the following code snippet. The parameterized function takes the *Unit* type of argument and returns *Int*. Specifying *Unit* is optional, so the *myMethod* signature can also be written as $myMethod(myArg :=> Int)$.

```
scala> def myMethod(myArg: () => Int) =
| println(myArg())
myMethod: (myArg: () => Int)Unit

scala> myMethod(() => 5)
5
```

When *myMethod* is called, the integer argument is not evaluated. It is evaluated at the time of printing because that is when it is needed. In a large industrial application there can be many memory-intensive operations in between function calls with functions as parameters and actual use of the values obtained by evaluating parameterized functions. If a parameterized function's evaluation demands significant memory then it is certainly helpful to delay the evaluation until the values are needed, because there are other operations that require memory and need to be executed in between.

1.3.2 Memoization

Memoization is a technique in which the results of previous calculations are stored so that they can be reused for future calculations. This clearly helps to avoid re-computing. In the case of a very large data set this is certainly going to save CPU time. Also, memoization is helpful even if local CPUs are not directly used. For example, if there are numerous web service calls that request the same information then those can be cached. This certainly improves the performance of the application. Now, let's walk through two implementations of factorial calculation—one without memoization and another with memoization.

```scala
scala> def calcFactorial(x: Int): Int = {
   |     if(x == 0 || x == 1)
   |        1
   |     else {
   |        println("Computing factorial")
   |        x * calcFactorial(x - 1)
   |     }
   | }
calcFactorial: (x: Int)Int
```

The code snippet above is a factorial calculation without memoization. It performs computation in every step, which can be seen in the following console output. Also, if we run *calcFactorial*(5) again we get the same console output, which confirms the re-computation.

```scala
scala> calcFactorial(5)
Computing factorial
Computing factorial
Computing factorial
Computing factorial
res5: Int = 120
```

Now, let's implement the same with memoization. In the code snippet below, we implement caching so that calculations performed earlier can be reused.

```scala
package com.equalinformation.dascala.scala
   .fundamentals

class FactorialMemoiz {
   var cache: Map[Int, Int] = Map()

   def lookup(num: Int): Int =
      cache.getOrElse(num, 0)

   def calcFactMemoiz(x: Int): Int = {
      if(x == 0 || x ==1)
```

```
                1
        else if(lookup(x) > 0) {
            println("Performing lookup")
            lookup(x)
        } else {
            println("Performing calculation")
            val factorial = x * calcFactMemoiz((x - 1))
            cache += x -> factorial
            factorial
        }
    }
}

object FactorialMemoizApp {
    def main(args: Array[String]): Unit = {
        val factMem = new FactorialMemoiz()
        println(factMem.calcFactMemoiz(3))
        println(factMem.calcFactMemoiz(5))
    }

}
```

Let's see the console output for this program. First the program calculated the factorial of 3, so it entered the calculation block twice. This calculation is stored in the cache. When we invoke the method to calculate the factorial for 6, it enters the calculation block twice for 5 and 4, whereas it gets the pre-computed value for 3, so we see one lookup. Caching-related questions are common in many software engineering job interviews. You might be asked to design and implement a caching strategy.

```
Performing calculation
Performing calculation
6
Performing calculation
Performing calculation
Performing lookup
120
```

1.4 Streams

In Section 1.3, we implemented both lazy evaluation and memoization. Fortunately, we don't have to implement those manually if we are using Scala's *Stream*, which is lazy, memoized, and immutable. This allows us to create infinite sequences using *Stream*. Now, let's look at *Stream* in action.

```
scala> val myStream = Stream("message1", "message2",
   "message3")
myStream: scala.collection.immutable.Stream[String]
   = Stream(message1, ?)
```

Even though we supplied three messages, only the first is listed, which means only the first element of the stream was computed. It is a lazy computation. Now, if we access an element at an index other than 0, it will force computation. Let's access the second element.

```
scala> myStream(1)
res7: String = message2

scala> myStream
res8: scala.collection.immutable.Stream[String] =
   Stream(message1, message2, ?)
```

It is evident that it has computed the second element as well. Also it is clear that it only computed until second element. So this is truly lazy computation. Now let's try a stream with a few more elements. For brevity, we use numbers.

```
scala> val myNums = Stream(0,1,2,3,4,5,6,7,8,9)
myNums: scala.collection.immutable.Stream[Int] =
   Stream(0, ?)

scala> myNums(3)
res9: Int = 3

scala> myNums
res10: scala.collection.immutable.Stream[Int] =
   Stream(0, 1, 2, 3, ?)

scala> myNums(9)
res11: Int = 9

scala> myNums
res12: scala.collection.immutable.Stream[Int] =
   Stream(0, 1, 2, 3, 4, 5, 6, 7, 8, 9, ?)
```

The code snippet above is intuitive. When we accessed the element at index 3, it automatically computed all elements until index 3. This is true when we accessed an element at index 9. Streams can also be create using the # :: operator. Let's see an example.

```
scala> val myStream = 'a' #:: 'b' #:: 'c' #:: 'd'
   #:: empty
myStream: scala.collection.immutable.Stream[Char] =
   Stream(a, ?)
```

So we can see that *Stream* behaves the same way. *empty* is an empty *Stream*. Let's
look at one more way of creating a stream, using the *cons* function.

```scala
scala> val myTestSteam = cons('a', empty)
myTestSteam: Stream.Cons[Char] = Stream(a, ?)
```

Infinite sequences are common in mathematics. They solve some of the most de-
manding computing problems like handling continuously generated log files, tweets,
etc. So let's create one sample infinite stream.

```scala
scala> def createInfStream(x: Int): Stream[Int] = {
     |     println("Processing...")
     |     cons(x, createInfStream(x + 1))
     | }
createInfStream: (x: Int)Stream[Int]
```

We created a function *createInfStream* that creates an infinite stream using *cons*.
It looks line an infinite loop, which is true. But the lazy nature of *Stream* makes it
computable, as it is on-demand computing. Now, let's access elements of the stream.

```scala
scala> val myInfIntStream = createInfStream(0)
Processing...
myInfIntStream: Stream[Int] = Stream(0, ?)

scala> myInfIntStream(0)
res15: Int = 0

scala> myInfIntStream(1)
Processing...
res16: Int = 1

scala> myInfIntStream(3)
Processing...
Processing...
res17: Int = 3

scala> myInfIntStream(5)
Processing...
Processing...
res18: Int = 5

scala> myInfIntStream(6)
Processing...
res19: Int = 6

scala> myInfIntStream(6)
res20: Int = 6
```

We can see that the computation is on-demand. When we invoked *createInfStream*, it created a stream with the first element. We accessed index 6 twice; the first time we accessed it, it was computed. When we accessed it a second time, it reused the pre-computed value. So it is lazy and memoized. Now, we need to try one more thing: immutability. Let's look at the following code snippet.

```scala
scala> var testImmInfStr = createInfStream(5)
Processing...
testImmInfStr: Stream[Int] = Stream(5, ?)

scala> testImmInfStr(4)
Processing...
Processing...
Processing...
Processing...
res22: Int = 9

scala> testImmInfStr(6)
Processing...
Processing...
res23: Int = 11

scala> testImmInfStr(5)
res24: Int = 10

scala> testImmInfStr(0)
res25: Int = 5

scala> testImmInfStr(3)
res27: Int = 8

scala> testImmInfStr(5) = 15
<console>:18: error: value update is not a member of
   Stream[Int]
testImmInfStr(5) = 15
  ^
```

Our starting value is 5. Then we accessed the element at index 4, which forced computation until index 4. That was true for index 6 as well, except it had to compute only two values, the remainder being reused. Next, when we accessed the element at index 5, it got a pre-calculated value; this was true for index 0 and index 3. Finally, we tried to assign a new value at index 5. Since *Stream* is immutable, it refused our request to update.

Now, let's quickly look at *Stream* to *List* conversion. In the case of infinite streams, we are trying to convert an infinite steam to a list. In this case, before converting, it tries to evaluate all of them, so evaluation never ends as it is an infinite list. So we need to be careful during stream to list conversion. There is a solution for this problem. Let's look at the code snippet below.

```scala
scala> testImmInfStr.take(5).toList
res28: List[Int] = List(5, 6, 7, 8, 9)

scala> testImmInfStr.toList
Processing...
Processing...
Processing...
Processing...
Processing...
Processing...
Processing...
Processing...
Processing...
Processing...
Processing...
Processing...
```

The first one terminates but the second one doesn't. What is the reason? In the first conversion, we limited the number of elements in the stream, which limited the evaluation and the computation terminated. In the second case, we gave an infinite set of numbers, so it kept evaluating those numbers first. Evaluation completes before conversion, which is the thing that we need to be careful about while converting a stream to a list.

Lastly, as an infinite series example, let's compute the Fibonacci series starting from 0. We define the function *createFiboSeries*, which takes the first two Fibonacci numbers. It is a recursive computation, so every time we iterate, the current second number becomes the new first number and the next number in the Fibonacci series is the sum of the current two numbers. The *cons* function prepends the first parameter, which is a single value in this case, to the second parameter, which is a stream, because *createFiboSeries* returns a stream of integers.

```scala
scala> def createFiboSeries(a: Int, b: Int):
  Stream[Int] = {
|    cons(a, createFiboSeries(b, a+b))
| }
createFiboSeries: (a: Int, b: Int)Stream[Int]

scala> val myFiboSeries = createFiboSeries(0, 1)
myFiboSeries: Stream[Int] = Stream(0, ?)

scala> myFiboSeries.take(7).foreach(println)
0
1
1
```

```
2
3
5
8
```

By using *take*(7), we limited our computation to the first seven Fibonacci numbers, which is how we terminated the infinite series. Then we applied *println* for each element in the series.

1.5 Sliding Windows

A sliding window enables us to break a list into smaller lists based on the window specification that we provide. The window-based chunks can be converted to other collections, such as arrays and vectors. On the surface, this might look like just a feature, but when used in the right context it gives us tools to model efficient solutions to a programming problem. A great solution, often, is a clever combination of basic tools. Next, let's look at a sliding window in action.

```scala
scala> val myNums = List(1,2,3,4,5,6,7,8,9)
myNums: List[Int] = List(1, 2, 3, 4, 5, 6, 7, 8, 9)

scala> myNums.sliding(2,1).toList
res9: List[List[Int]] = List(List(1, 2), List(2, 3),
    List(3, 4), List(4, 5), List(5, 6), List(6, 7),
    List(7, 8), List(8, 9))

scala> myNums.sliding(3,1).toList
res10: List[List[Int]] = List(List(1, 2, 3),
    List(2, 3, 4), List(3, 4, 5), List(4, 5, 6),
    List(5, 6, 7), List(6, 7, 8), List(7, 8, 9))

scala> myNums.sliding(1,2).toList
res11: List[List[Int]] = List(List(1), List(3),
    List(5), List(7), List(9))

scala> myNums.sliding(1,3).toList
res12: List[List[Int]] = List(List(1), List(4),
    List(7))

scala> myNums.sliding(1,4).toList
res13: List[List[Int]] = List(List(1), List(5),
    List(9))

scala> myNums.sliding(5,1).toList
```

```
res14: List[List[Int]] = List(List(1, 2, 3, 4, 5),
   List(2, 3, 4, 5, 6), List(3, 4, 5, 6, 7),
   List(4, 5, 6, 7, 8), List(5, 6, 7, 8, 9))

scala> myNums.sliding(5,5).toList
res15: List[List[Int]] = List(List(1, 2, 3, 4, 5),
   List(6, 7, 8, 9))

scala> myNums.sliding(5,4).toList
res16: List[List[Int]] = List(List(1, 2, 3, 4, 5),
   List(5, 6, 7, 8, 9))
```

Does this code snippet give you a clue as to how it works? You cannot get it wrong if you are applying this to petabytes of data; thousands of reports can go wrong if you make a mistake with this simple but powerful feature. The signature of the *sliding* method is *sliding(size: Int, step: Int): Iterator[List[A]]*, where *size* is the number of elements per group and *step* is the distance between the first elements of successive groups.

Let's look at the first six lines (a blank line doesn't count). We have a list containing numbers from 1 to 9. Our sliding window size is 2, which means we are telling the compiler that substructures should have two elements in them. Our step size is 1, which means the first element of the first sublist and the first element of the second sublist should be consecutive elements. When *myNums.sliding(2,3).toList* is executed, what will the first element of the second sublist be? The answer is 4, because sublists can contain only two elements, and the distance should be 3 for consecutive first elements of sublists. The time complexity of a sliding window operation specified by $sliding(2,1)$ is $O(n)$. Since we need to store elements in the sublists, we need space proportional to the input elements, so the space complexity is also $O(n)$.

Exercise 1.2. *Time and Space Complexity for* $sliding(x,y)$

Find the time and space complexity for the sliding window operations. Assume that input data can be of any size and length.

1. *sliding(3, 1)*
2. *sliding(1, 2)*
3. *sliding(1, 3)*
4. *sliding(1, 4)*
5. *sliding(5, 1)*
6. *sliding(5, 5)*
7. *sliding(5, 4)*
8. *x.sliding(1, x.size)*
9. *x.sliding(x.size, 1)*
10. *x.sliding((x.size) / 2, 1)*

11. *x.sliding(1, (x.size) / 2)*

Chapter 2
Fundamental Algorithms

Clarity is the most important thing in order to get the best out of any discipline. For data structures and algorithms, wrong choices can easily waste millions of dollars (convert this to your currency of interest). A small mistake can easily waste thousands of dollars. In this context, it is important to have a sound understanding of the fundamentals of the discipline in context. For us, fundamental algorithms give insight and clarity on how to use the building blocks correctly and optimally. This is the theme of this chapter. In order to gain better clarity and sound understanding of data structures and algorithms, we will visit several fundamental algorithms.

2.1 Prime Numbers

A prime number is defined as a number that is only divisible by itself and one, excluding one. It is an infinite sequence: $< 2,3,5,7,11,13,17,19,23,29,31,37,41,43,47,... >$. One of the popular applications of prime numbers is cryptography. Prime numbers are also used in hash functions to avoid collision, in random numbers generators for uniform distribution, and in error-correcting code for noise elimination.

First, let's outline an algorithm to generate prime numbers:

1. Create a container containing all the numbers greater than or equal to 2. This is where we find all the prime numbers.
2. Limit the range if working with a finite computing resources like memory and processing power so as to make it computationally feasible.
3. Apply prime number detection logic to each number, x:

    a. Create a list of numbers that are less than or equal to the square root of the number, x. $R = \{y_1, y_2, ..., y_n\}$, where $y_1 < y_2 < ... < y_n$ and $y_n <= squareRoot(x)$. The function $squareRoot(x)$ produces the square root of the integer x.

© Springer Nature Switzerland AG 2019
B. P. Upadhyaya, *Data Structures and Algorithms with Scala*, Undergraduate Topics in Computer Science, https://doi.org/10.1007/978-3-030-12561-5_2

b. Divide x by each numbers in the square root list, R, and see if the remainder is zero in any one of the cases. If so, then exclude x from the list of primes; otherwise add it to the list.

4. Return the computed list.

```
package com.equalinformation.dascala.scala.fundamentals

object PrimeNumbersApp {
   def main(args: Array[String]): Unit = {
      println(primes.take(15).toList)
   }

   val primes: Stream[Int] = 2 #:: Stream.from(3)
      .filter {
         x => {
            val sqrtOfPrimes = primes.takeWhile(y =>
               y <= math.sqrt(x))
            !sqrtOfPrimes.exists( y => x % y == 0)
         }
      }
}

// Output: List(2, 3, 5, 7, 11, 13, 17, 19, 23, 29, 31, 37,
// 41, 43, 47)
```

Fig. 2.1: Prime number generation using *Stream*

In Figure 2.1, we present a program to generate prime numbers. *primes* is a stream of integers and is capable representing an infinite series. In our case, it does represent an infinite series of integers. We generate it by combining the first element of the series with a lazily evaluated stream, as shown in the code. Next, we need to filter all non-primes. How do we do this? One way of doing it is to divide the number x by numbers between 2 and $(x-1)$ and see if there is a remainder in one of those divisions. If there is a remainder in one of those divisions then it is not a prime, otherwise it is. This is correct logic but it is not efficient.

Alternatively, as seen above, we can calculate the square root of the number x and divide it by the numbers from 2 to its square root and see if there is remainder in any one of those divisions. If there is a remainder then x is not a prime, otherwise it is a prime. This is more efficient logic than the previous one and hence we implement this logic in Figure 2.1.

Exercise 2.1. *Time and Space Complexity*

For the solution presented in Figure 2.1, calculate the time and space complexity. You may want to refer Section B.3 for asymptotic notations.

2.2 Decimal to Binary Conversion

We are converting base 10 numbers to base 2 numbers. In these two number systems, counting procedure differs mainly because of the symbols used. Let's outline the conversion algorithm, first.

1. Staring from the given number, create a sequence of numbers in such a way that the succeeding number is half of the previous number, discarding the decimal portion. Continue this until the last element satisfies $2 > x > 0$, where x is the last number in the sequence. Formally, $S = \{x_1, x_2, ..., x_n\}$, where $x_2 = x_1/2$, $x_3 = x_2/2$ and so on, and $2 > x_n > 0$.
2. For each number in the above list, divide by 2 and store the remainder in a container.
3. The container now contains the binary equivalent bits in reverse order, $b_1 b_2...b_n$, so reverse the order to get the binary equivalent number, $b_n...b_2 b_1$.

Now, let's implement the above algorithm. In Figure 2.2, we present a typical implementation.

```
package com.equalinformation.dascala.scala.fundamentals

object DecimalToBinaryConvApp {
   def main(args: Array[String]): Unit = {
      println(decToBinConv(5))
      println(decToBinConv(8))
   }

   def decToBinConv(x: Int): String = {
      val seqOfDivByTwo = Iterator.iterate(x)(a => a / 2)
      val binList = seqOfDivByTwo.takeWhile(a => a > 0)
        .map(a => a % 2)
      binList.mkString.reverse
   }
}
```

Fig. 2.2: Decimal to binary conversion using *Iterator*

The *decToBinConv* method takes a decimal number and converts it to its binary equivalent. How does it do it? First, it creates a sequence of numbers by dividing the given number by 2 until it is less than 2. It collects the quotient. Next, it divides each number in that sequence by 2 and stores the remainder in the collection *binList*, which is an iterator of *Int*. The bits are accumulated in this container in reverse order, and hence the last LOC reverses the order, converting the iterator into a string before that.

Exercise 2.2. *Lazy Evaluation, and Time and Space Complexity*

For the solution presented in Figure 2.2,

- explain where lazy evaluation is taking place, and
- calculate the time and space complexity.

You may want to refer Section B.3 for asymptotic notations.

2.3 Divide and Conquer

Some problems appear complex as a whole. The same problem, when broken down into smaller subproblems is easier to solve. The solutions to subproblems can be combined to get the global solution to the problem. This is known as, divide and conquer, which is a widely used technique in computer science problem solving. We will see in Chapter 9 how this technique helps to achieve better performance. Also, divide and conquer can be used to solve big data problems. In some companies, data are already distributed; in this context, we can take computing close to these distributed data, get the local results and combine them to form global results. If data are not already distributed, then we divide data so that they can be processed in pieces. Then the results from those pieces can be merged to form the final solution. We've already discussed how divide and conquer works; now, let's outline the algorithm, just for formality.

1. Divide the problem into smaller subproblems.
2. Find problem-specific solution to the subproblems.
3. Merge the solutions of the subproblems to form the final solution.

Now, let's take a problem and apply our algorithmic outline to find a solution. Let's assume that you are a student, currently studying computer science. Your parents send tuition money to your account at the beginning of each semester. Your school allows you to pay your tuition toward the end of the semester on a request basis. Let's assume that school is not strict about your reason as long as you pay the tuition before the semester ends. Close to the computer science department, there is a superb restaurant run by special arrangement between your university and the restaurant chain owner. On a daily basis, the restaurant offers food items from every major culture in the world. That means, today you can eat at Berlin, and tomorrow you can eat at Tokyo. You stay late in the labs doing a lot of programming so that you don't have time to cook yourself. The restaurant is a perfect solution for you, except for one thing: money. It is a bit expensive and your pocket money is not enough to buy food everyday, specially if you want to buy from this restaurant on a regular basis.

As a very bright computer science student, you figured out the solution based on your tuition money, i.e., your tuition money stays in your account most of the semester, before it leaves as a tuition payment in the last week of the semester. You have the opportunity to invest this money and make some profit to buy your food from the restaurant. You figured out that buying and selling stock is your best option as a short-term investor. But you also figured out that you need to be really clever to make money out of stock trading, specially as you cannot afford to lose significant money because you must pay your tuition fee at the end of the semester. So you are looking for the maximum stock value in a window so that you can plan for your future trading.

Table 2.1 shows your recordings of stocks for two weeks, on consecutive business days. A window can be as large as the entire two weeks or it can be a single day. As a smart computer science student, you figured out that creating a difference table makes it easy to find such a maximum window. Very quickly, you realized that this is a maximum subarray problem. Also, based on your *Data Structure and Algorithm* course, you came to know that divide and conquer gives an *n lg n* solution, instead of a brute force solution, which has $O(n^2)$ running time complexity. You decided to implement a divide and conquer-based solution. Coincidentally, you got hold of this book and found that Figure 2.3 presents the solution that you were trying to implement on your own. Let's discuss this solution next.

Table 2.1: Sample stock price data

Day	0	1	2	3	4	5	6	7	8	9	10
Stock Price	$150	$151	$149	$154	$160	$159	$163	$172	$169	$171	$176
Difference		1	-2	5	6	-1	4	9	-3	2	5

In Figure 2.3, the method *leftRightCrossMax* computes the sum of the maximum of the left subarray sums and the maximum of the right subarray sums. The method *findContSubArrayMax* calculates the sum of the maximum producing continuous subarray, which is the maximum stock price increase. It takes a vector of integers and returns an integer, which is the sum that we are interested in. In order to compute this maximum subarray-based sum, it does pattern matching on the input data, *data*. If the input data contains only a single value, then that is the answer. Otherwise, the input vector is split into two from the middle. Then a recursive call is made to break down the left split as well as the right split until no more splitting is required. When no more splitting is required, it computes back. Along with finding the left maximum and the right maximum, we also find the cross maximum. Finally we take the maximum of the left maximum, right maximum, and cross maximum, which is

```scala
package com.equalinformation.dascala.scala.fundamentals

object MaxContSubArrayApp {
  def main(args: Array[String]): Unit = {
    val stockPriceDiff = Vector(1, -2, 5, 6, -1, 4, 9, -3,
      2, 5)
    println(findContSubArrayMax(stockPriceDiff))
  }

  def findContSubArrayMax(data: Vector[Int]): Int =
    data match {
    case Vector(x) => x
    case _ => {
      val (l, r) = data.splitAt(data.length / 2)
      val leftMax = findContSubArrayMax(l)
      val rightMax  = findContSubArrayMax(r)
      val leftRightCrossMaxVal = leftRightCrossMax(l,r)
      List(leftMax, rightMax, leftRightCrossMaxVal).max
    }
  }

  def leftRightCrossMax(leftSub: Vector[Int], rightSub:
    Vector[Int]): Int = {
    val collLeftSums = for(i <- 1 to leftSub.length) yield
      leftSub.takeRight(i).sum
    val collRightSums = for(i <- 1 to rightSub.length) yield
      rightSub.take(i).sum
    collLeftSums.max + collRightSums.max
  }
}
```

Fig. 2.3: Maximum continuous subarray sum: divide and conquer

the maximum value that we are interested in. You can test the program with a wide variety of input data.

2.4 Greedy Algorithms

Greedy algorithms use the strategy of making the most profitable local selections in the hope of finding the most profitable global selection. This means that in every iteration we will be looking for the best local choice, which is the most beneficial. Let's take a problem and see how it works for us.

Let's assume that you have colorful spring garden flowers and you want to protect them from deer, children, rabbits, poultry, dogs, etc. Your garden is of rectangular shape and you have calculated the perimeter using formula $P = 2(l + b)$. You did a quick search on Amazon and found most cost-effective garden safety netting material made of metal. You decided to go with metal for its strength and durability. You also found that buying larger pieces gives you a cost advantage and saves you from doing additional joint work. You realize that joining nets is hard as well as costly. Now we need to find an algorithm for you to buy the right numbers and combinations of pieces of safety nets. Let's assume that you want to use this algorithm as well as the corresponding program for your future garden as well, which is likely to be of different dimensions. Also, at that time, Amazon might show different dimensions for netting materials. In this context, we would like to write a generic algorithm and provide a generic implementation as well.

```
package com.equalinformation.dascala.scala.fundamentals

case class Selection(perimeter: Int, gardenNets: List[Int])

object GardenNettingGreedyAlgoApp {
   def main(args: Array[String]): Unit = {
      val gardenNetLengths = Array(15,10,3,2,1)
      val perimeter = 50
      println(selectNets(perimeter, gardenNetLengths))
   }

   def selectNets(perimeter: Int, netLengths: Array[Int]):
     List[Int] = {
      val finalSelection = netLengths.foldLeft(Selection(
        perimeter, List())) {
        (selection, length) => {
           val numbers = selection.perimeter / length
           val netsToBuy = List.fill(numbers)(length)
           Selection(selection.perimeter - numbers * length,
             selection.gardenNets ::: netsToBuy)
        }
      }
      finalSelection.gardenNets
   }
}
```

Fig. 2.4: Garden safety netting: greedy algorithm

In Figure 2.4, we provide a generic implementation for you to assist in making your garden netting material purchase decision. Next, let's discuss the implementation. The method *selectNets* takes the perimeter and available netting material lengths as its arguments, and returns a list of netting material combinations. For example, if it recommends two pieces of material with length 15 units then it returns $\{15,15\}$. We make use of fold left here. For each pair of selection and length, *numbers* is calculated by dividing *perimeter* by *length*, the quotient giving the number of pieces to buy. Of course, we start with the highest, because that saves cost for you. For this, we supply the suitably sorted, descending order, array of lengths. Then we fill a list those many times with the current value of *length*. So this gives us how many pieces to buy for a given length. Next, we create our *Selection* object, which holds our data. The distance left is obtained by subtracting product of *numbers* and the current *length* from *perimeter*. The second parameter in our case class is a list of pieces, initially empty. In the first iteration, it is obtained by prepending *netsToBuy* to the empty list created during object creation. Finally, we return *gardenNets*, which contains the recommendation, i.e., how many pieces of what length. The console output for our implementation, in Figure 2.4, is $List(15,15,15,3,2)$. This completes our discussion of this garden fencing greedy algorithm implementation.

Exercise 2.3. *Garden safety netting: algorithm reverse engineering*

In industrial programming, it sometimes happens that somebody else writes the algorithms and implements them. Over a period of time the documentation for algorithms is lost and only executable programs are available. The source of information for new engineers joining the teams is business information through meetings with different stakeholders and the source code repository. Often, it is true that information provided in the meetings is vague. In this context, your best bet to find the corresponding algorithms is to reverse engineer the implementation. Keeping that in mind, we ask you do a preparatory exercise here. For the implementation in Figure 2.4, document the corresponding algorithm by reverse engineering the code.

Chapter 3
Arrays

The *Oxford English Dictionary* (OED) defines an array as "an ordered series or arrangement," for example, an array of solar panels, an array of pixels, etc. The OED's mathematics version of the definition is "an arrangement of quantities or symbols in rows and columns; a matrix," whereas the computing version of the definition is "an indexed set of related elements." All three definitions agree on ordering the entities in context. So an array is an ordered structure. The three versions also give us a hint about how to map a computing specific structure to a mathematical structure, and finally to a real world structure.

Not all ordered arrangements may be easily analyzed using mathematics. For example, the layers in our body are ordered arrangements and if we try to construct a mathematical model it will probably be complex, specially if we want to deal at the cellular depth and beyond. Similarly, not all symbols in rows and columns may be computationally feasible. To be specific, in mathematics, it is fairly convenient to model something approaching infinity because it is a thought process, and we can symbolize that thought process with standard notations, methods, rules, etc. But in the case of computers, we have limited memory and processing power. A great deal of data structures and algorithms problems are related to this fact. If we are getting harder problems in job interviews, that probably has something to do with this reality, which is independent of domains.

Whether we work in finance, biotechnology, education, government, or energy, this problem appears uniformly. This is also the origin of something called *Abstract Data Types*. Arrays are not particularly abstract, but we will be dealing with ADTs later in this book. An array is more like a foundational data structure that can be utilized to implement other data structures, which are more abstract in nature. The ADTs build a bridge between real-world and computing infrastructures. One of the types of computing infrastructure is the programming language. Almost all the high-level programming languages provide a mechanism to express arrays. Scala is close to mathematics compared to many other high-level programming languages available today, and hence makes it more convenient to express and process arrays.

© Springer Nature Switzerland AG 2019
B. P. Upadhyaya, *Data Structures and Algorithms with Scala*, Undergraduate
Topics in Computer Science, https://doi.org/10.1007/978-3-030-12561-5_3

3.1 Structure

We will try to use as much mathematics as possible while trying to express structures, as it is closer to computing. It is a lot more convenient to transform a mathematical structure to a computer program, provided the model or structure is computationally feasible. An array can be expressed as a sequence: $< a_0, a_1, ..., a_n >$, where n is a positive integer greater than 1. The subscripts are the indices. One of the instances of this generic sequence is $< a, e, i, o, u >$ or $< a, e, ..., u >$. In this case, $n = 5$. We can access the third vowel with the help of its corresponding index. If we name this sequence as V, then $V_3 = i$, provided indexing starts at 1. We could use notation like $V[3]$, $V(3)$, or $third(V)$. If the indexing starts at 0 then the representation is $V_2 = i$. Different programming languages use different styles to represent an array.

Reading as well as modifying an element at a given index, i, takes $O(1)$ time. Inserting an element at the ith position requires $(n - i)$ shifting and hence it is $O(n - i)$; similarly, deleting an element at i^{th} index takes $O(n - i)$ time. Inserting an element into a full array requires creating a new array with higher capacity, copying all the elements of the old array, and inserting the new element.

Next, let's look at how Scala enables us to express array processing.

```scala
scala> val vowels = Array('a', 'e', 'i', 'o', 'u')
vowels: Array[Char] = Array(a, e, i, o, u)

scala> vowels(2)
res0: Char = i

scala> val vowelsReversed = vowels.reverse
vowelsReversed: Array[Char] = Array(u, o, i, e, a)

scala> vowelsReversed(2)
res1: Char = i

scala> vowels.length
res4: Int = 5
```

The code snippet above shows how to create an array containing vowels. The third vowel is accessed using its index, i.e., *vowels*(2), indexing starts at 0. Next, we call a library method to reverse the contents of the array *vowels* and assign reversed contents to a new constant called *vowelsReversed*. Since the position of *i* remains same, *vowelsReversed*(2) gives us the same value. Next, we get the length of *vowels*; the length of *vowelsReversed* must be equal.

Exercise 3.1. *Implement the length method*

Implement a method or a function called *calcLength* that is functionally equivalent to the *length* method shown in the code snippet above, without using built-in library methods; you are only allowed to use the basic control structures available in Scala. Also calculate the time complexity. You can either implement a single method in REPL and test, or create a complete application using the IDE or tool of your choice. Hint: you can use a terminator. A solution is available in Section A.1, which contains a complete application.

3.2 Typical Implementation

Let's take a problem of matrix multiplication in order to illustrate array deployment or implementation. Equation 3.1 has three matrices; the first one is 2×3 and the second one is 3×4, which gives the dimension of the resultant matrix as 2×4.

$$\begin{bmatrix} 2.5 & 1.5 & 0.5 \\ 1 & 2 & 4 \end{bmatrix} \begin{bmatrix} -1 & -1.5 & 1 & -1 \\ 0.5 & -2 & -2.5 & 1 \\ 1 & 2 & 1 & 1 \end{bmatrix} = \begin{bmatrix} -1.25 & -5.75 & -0.75 & -0.5 \\ 4.0 & 2.5 & 0.0 & 5.0 \end{bmatrix} \quad (3.1)$$

In order to write a program for matrix multiplication, we need to remind ourselves a few rules of matrix multiplication:

- The number of columns in the first matrix should be equal to the number of rows in the second matrix.
- The resultant matrix will have dimensions such that the number of rows is equal to the number of rows of the first matrix and the number of columns is equal to the number of columns of the second matrix.

Now, let's outline our algorithm. We will use pseudocode and traditional mathematical notation to outline our algorithms throughout this book.

1. Define matrix multiplication logic for matrices A and B.

   a. Allocate space for the resultant matrix, C.
   b. Calculate the lengths of the rows and columns of two given matrices. Let's call them *mat1Rows* or p, *mat1Columns* or r, *mat2Rows* or r, and mat2Columns or q.
   c. *if* (*mat1Columns* $\neq$ *mat2Rows*) then print an error message stating that the given matrices don't satisfy a matrix multiplication rule.
   d. Else, compute the resultant matrix
      i. Design variables for calculation: i is an integer variable denoting rows in A where $0 < i \leq p$, j is an integer variable denoting columns in B where $0 < j \leq q$, and k is an integer variable denoting columns in A and rows in B where $(0 < k \leq mat1Columns) \wedge (0 < k \leq mat2Rows)$.

ii. $C_{11} = A_{11} * B_{11} + A_{12} * B_{21} + A_{13} * B_{31},$
$C_{12} = A_{11} * B_{12} + A_{12} * B_{22} + A_{13} * B_{32},$
$C_{13} = A_{11} * B_{13} + A_{12} * B_{23} + A_{13} * B_{33},$
$C_{14} = A_{11} * B_{14} + A_{12} * B_{24} + A_{13} * B_{34},$
$C_{21} = A_{21} * B_{11} + A_{22} * B_{21} + A_{23} * B_{31},$
$C_{22} = A_{21} * B_{12} + A_{22} * B_{22} + A_{23} * B_{32},$
$C_{23} = A_{21} * B_{13} + A_{22} * B_{23} + A_{23} * B_{33},$
$C_{24} = A_{21} * B_{14} + A_{22} * B_{24} + A_{23} * B_{34}$

iii. Find patterns and generalize the previous step, which gives us the following relation to calculate the resultant matrix.

$$C = \bigsqcup_{i=1}^{p} \bigsqcup_{j=1}^{q} \sum_{k=1}^{r} A_{ik} * B_{kj} \tag{3.2}$$

2. In the main routine, define matrices A and B.
3. Call the matrix multiplication subroutine, defined earlier.

In Figure 3.1, we present an application that implements the above algorithmic outline. The matrix multiplication subroutine is implemented as the method *multiplyMatrices*, which takes two arguments, each a two-dimensional matrix. Its return type is also a two-dimensional matrix. The body of this method first allocates space for the resultant matrix, *resultMat*; the dimensions are calculated based on the input parameters. Next, the method calculates the dimensions of the input matrices so that they can be used as upper limits. There is a quick validation of matrix rules, which should be satisfied in order to proceed the computation. The *for* loops implement the relation that we found after detecting patterns in our detail steps above. Finally, the method returns the result.

In the main method, first we define two matrices A and B as *myMatrix*1 and *myMatrix*2, respectively. Next, we call the subroutine by passing matrices A and B; the result is assigned to a constant *myResultMatrix*. Finally, we print each element of the resultant matrix for validation.

```scala
package com.equalinformation.dascala.scala.arrays

object MatrixMultApp {
    def main(args: Array[String]): Unit = {
        val myMatrix1: Array[Array[Double]] = Array(Array(2.5,
         1.5, 0.5), Array(1, 2, 4))
        val myMatrix2: Array[Array[Double]] = Array(Array(-1,
         -1.5, 1, -1), Array(0.5, -2, -2.5, 1), Array(1, 2,
         1, 1))
        val myResultMatrix: Array[Array[Double]] =
         multiplyMatrices(myMatrix1, myMatrix2)

        for(i <- 0 until myResultMatrix.length ) {
            for(j <- 0 until myResultMatrix(0).length) {
                println(myResultMatrix(i)(j)+ " ")
            }
            println()
        }
    }

    def multiplyMatrices(mat1: Array[Array[Double]],
     mat2: Array[Array[Double]]): Array[Array[Double]] = {
        var resultMat = Array.ofDim[Double](mat1.length,
         mat2(0).length)

        val mat1Rows = mat1.length
        val mat1Columns = mat1(0).length
        val mat2Rows = mat2.length
        val mat2Columns = mat2(0).length

        if(mat1Columns != mat2Rows) {
            println("Matrix 1 columns: " + mat1Columns +
             " did not match with Matrix 2 rows: " + mat2Rows)
        } else {
            for(i <- 0 until mat1Rows) {
                for(j <- 0 until mat2Columns) {
                    for(k <- 0 until mat1Columns) {
                        resultMat(i)(j) += mat1(i)(k) * mat2(k)(j)
                    }
                }
            }
        }

        resultMat
    }
}
```

Fig. 3.1: Matrix multiplication

3.3 Analysis

The implementation presented in Figure 3.1 has three *for* loops. The innermost *for* loop takes care of the number of columns in the first matrix and the number of rows in the second matrix. This is clearly dependent on the input matrices and hence $O(mat1Columns)$ time, i.e., as the length of the columns of the first matrix increases, the computation time also increases. The same holds true for the length of the rows of the second matrix.

The middle loop takes care of the length of the columns of the second matrix, which in turn takes care of the length of the columns of the resultant matrix. So the computation time is directly proportional to the length of the columns of the second matrix. Hence we can say that it takes $O(mat2Columns)$ time to take care of this part of the computation. Similarly, it takes $O(mat1Rows)$ to take care of external row-based computation, which gives the length of the rows of the resultant matrix.

We can approximate $mat1Columns$, $mat2Columns$, and $mat1Rows$ to n. With this approximation, the time complexity of our implementation is $O(n^3)$. In practice, we might get row-based data or column-based data. Row-based data can have a very large number of rows and a very small number of columns. If there are billions of rows and only a few columns, we need to re-analyze that context to come up with a better big O approximation. We might need well-tailored solutions in such cases. Row-based and column-based databases are practical examples, even though database rows and columns might need to go through multiple transformations before they become arrays, internally.

Exercise 3.2. *Improve Matrix Multiplication*

The solution presented in Figure 3.1 has time complexity of $O(n^3)$. Can you think of a matrix multiplication algorithm that has better time complexity than $O(n^3)$? Consider these aspects of matrix-based data: (a) well-balanced, (b) row-heavy, (c) column-heavy, and (d) mixed.

3.4 Application

Arrays, as you will see, are widely used to implement other data structures. Almost every other data structure utilizes arrays in one form or another. You are also likely to find arrays or their equivalents in almost every high level-programming language. Not only that, you can find array-equivalent structures in assembly language and hardware itself. For example, a memory can be though of as a two-dimensional array of bits. For this reason, when higher performance is needed, it is convenient to fall back to array structures.

Numerous teams around the world are doing research on array-based databases [DMB16] [SS18] [SCMMS18]. This is evidence of the importance of arrays. One of the array-oriented databases is SciDB [Sci18]. Extensive array-based benchmarking is shown in [CMMK$^+$18], including superior performance over MySQL. The factors contributing to the superior performance are listed as direct offsetting and omission of index attributes, which are enabled by array-oriented data model; column-oriented design and separate storage of each attribute; data partitioning to facilitate both parallel and sequential computation. [Sto18] presents an overview of big data landscape, in which he emphasizes the importance of array-oriented databases. The author also claims that eventually *column stores* will win the race in the database world.

Big data analytics and its applications, including machine learning, clustering, and trend detection, are heavy on quantitative analysis. Most of the analytics operations are specified as linear algebra on array data. Matrices are heavily utilized in big data applications; we have dealt with one of the important matrix operations.

Exercise 3.3. *Discuss an Array-Oriented Database*

Discuss an array-oriented database. Based on your research, explain why the array-approach was chosen.

Exercise 3.4. *Dynamic Array Creation Based on Available System Memory*

Calculate the total available system memory and create an array to occupy that memory. Next, create an elastic array to utilize half of the available memory and gradually occupy the rest of the available memory, dynamically, i.e., checking the availability of the second half of the previously available memory in real time. This array should also be capable of shrinking to release memory to other applications.

Exercise 3.5. *Control Structure Transformation*

Analyze the following AQL statement, which looks similar to a typical SQL statement:

```
CREATE ARRAY MyArray
   < A: integer NULLS,
      B: double,
      C: USER_DEFINED_TYPE >
```

```
[ I=0:999999, 10000, 100, J=0:999999, 10000,
  100 ]
PARTITION OVER ( Node1, Node2, Node3 )
USING block_cyclic();
```

Note the structure inside the pair of square brackets. This is a control structure, which has structural similarities to some of the Scala control structures. One that might seem very close is the Scala *for* expression. Now, write a Scala application that takes this AQL control structure as an input and transforms it to a Scala *for* expression, which is an output for your application. In the AQL above, I and J provide range, 10000 (a number after the range) specifies chunk size, and 100 (a number after the chunk size) specifies overlap. If you need additional information about AQL, refer to the SciDB documentation online [Sci18].

Chapter 4
Lists

We make lists of things in our daily life. They are a way of keeping things together so that they can be tracked, processed, or managed. If we are working for large corporations, we have a list of employees, a list of contractors, a list of applications, a list of buildings, a list of cafeterias, etc. The list of employees can be further divided into sublists based on their groups or categories, for example, a list of managerial employees, a list of engineering employees, a list of information technology employees, etc. Similarly, a list of buildings can be divided into a list of owned building, a list of leased buildings, and so on. It is hard to live a life without lists. So this answers the question why lists?

It is quite obvious from the above that there is a need for grouping information in the form of lists or splitting information in the form of sublists. Sometimes we need an aggregated report and at other times we need more specialized reports. This creates the need for merging and splitting lists based on criteria. How many criteria can there be? It is hard to answer this question without knowing the business. Even after knowing the current state of business, it is hard to list complete criteria, as the business can change. So instead of listing exhaustive criteria, we abstract out common operations and treat them as software engineering processes.

From a software engineering point of view, we don't care whether it is a list of doctors or a list of engineers working for a company. If we are dealing with a list of names, from the computational perspective the things we need to care are: *What makes a valid name? What are the allowed structures in the names? How can names be composed? Do names contain only letters or numbers as well?* It doesn't matter whether it is an engineer's name or a doctor's name. But from a business perspective that might matter. So there is a dual presence of independence, which is what creates design challenges.

© Springer Nature Switzerland AG 2019
B. P. Upadhyaya, *Data Structures and Algorithms with Scala*, Undergraduate Topics in Computer Science, https://doi.org/10.1007/978-3-030-12561-5_4

4.1 Structure

Based on our needs, the information can be modeled in the form of a list structure. Thus structure is guided by what we need. Since final computation is done in a machine or multiple machines, the structure is partly influenced by how the machines operate. So limitations can be imposed by computational devices. Let's model a few real-world lists in order to come with some structures.

Let's say we need to maintain a list of company employees with relevant information. So an employee is a thing for us. Let's make further assumptions and say that relevant information about the employee in this context is the employee's first name, last name, department, group, and salary. All other information, except salary, is composed of alphabetical characters. Salary is expressed as a decimal number. Now, we can formally model this information.

$$Thing \stackrel{def}{=\!=} \{Employee\}$$
$$Employee \stackrel{def}{=\!=} \{first\ name,\ last\ name,\ department,\ group,\ salary\}$$
$$or$$
$$Employee \stackrel{def}{=\!=} \{name,\ department,\ group,\ salary\}$$

High-level programming languages have something called type. Information is modeled with the help of this type so that different features based on type theory can be applied to catch and correct common mistakes programmers make. Now, let's try to go one step closer to programming languages. *Employee* can be represented as a type and can have attributes. So the next level of modeling can be:

$$type = Employee$$
$$attributes = name,\ department,\ group,\ salary$$

In the next section, we will use Scala to implement our models. Further, we might need operators that enable us to process our list of employees. We need operators to aggregate multiple lists, to split a list, to retrieve an element from a list, to delete an element in the list, and so on. We will not bother about defining those here; if we do, we will end up developing a programming language, which is out of the scope of this book.

4.2 Typical Implementation

In Scala, a type like *Employee*, in the previous section, can be expressed as a case class. Let's look at the following code snippet.

```scala
scala> abstract class Employee(firstName: String,
  lastName: String, department: String,
  salary: Double)
```

```
defined class Employee

scala> case class Engineer(firstName: String,
  lastName: String, department: String, salary: Double,
  group: String) extends Employee(firstName, lastName,
  department, salary)
defined class Engineer

scala> case class Doctor(firstName: String,
  lastName: String, department: String, salary: Double,
  group: String) extends Employee(firstName, lastName,
  department, salary)
defined class Doctor

scala> val eng1 = Engineer("Isaac", "Newton", "IT",
  4500.50, "Engineering")
eng1: Engineer = Engineer(Isaac,Newton,IT,4500.5,
  Engineering)

scala> val eng2 = Engineer("Albert", "Einstein",
  "Infra", 4600.50, "Engineering")
eng2: Engineer = Engineer(Albert,Einstein,Infra,
  4600.5,Engineering)

scala> val doc1 = Doctor("Michael","Young","Cardio",
  5000.5,"Medicine")
doc1: Doctor = Doctor(Michael,Young,Cardio,5000.5,
  Medicine)

scala> val doc2 = Doctor("Jeffrey","Hall","Pathology",
  5100.5,"Medicine")
doc2: Doctor = Doctor(Jeffrey,Hall,Pathology,5100.5,
  Medicine)

scala> val engineers = List(eng1,eng2)
engineers: List[Engineer] = List(Engineer(Isaac,
  Newton,IT,4500.5,Engineering), Engineer(Albert,
  Einstein,Infra,4600.5,Engineering))

scala> val doctors = List(doc1,doc2)
doctors: List[Doctor] = List(Doctor(Michael,Young,
  Cardio,5000.5,Medicine), Doctor(Jeffrey,Hall,
  Pathology,5100.5,Medicine))

scala> val employees = engineers ::: doctors
```

```
employees: List[Product with Serializable with
 Employee] = List(Engineer(Isaac,Newton,IT,4500.5,
 Engineering), Engineer(Albert,Einstein,Infra,4600.5,
 Engineering), Doctor(Michael,Young,Cardio,5000.5,
 Medicine), Doctor(Jeffrey,Hall,Pathology,5100.5,
 Medicine))

scala> val emp2 = List(engineers, doctors)
emp2: List[List[Product with Serializable with
 Employee]] = List(List(Engineer(Isaac,Newton,IT,
 4500.5,Engineering), Engineer(Albert,Einstein,Infra,
 4600.5,Engineering)), List(Doctor(Michael,Young,
 Cardio,5000.5,Medicine), Doctor(Jeffrey,Hall,
 Pathology,5100.5,Medicine)))

scala> emp2.flatten
res0: List[Product with Serializable with Employee] =
 List(Engineer(Isaac,Newton,IT,4500.5,Engineering),
 Engineer(Albert,Einstein,Infra,4600.5,Engineering),
 Doctor(Michael,Young,Cardio,5000.5,Medicine),
 Doctor(Jeffrey,Hall,Pathology,5100.5,Medicine))

scala> engineers.size
res4: Int = 2

scala> doctors.size
res5: Int = 2

scala> employees.size
res6: Int = 4

scala> employees.exists(x => x == eng1)
res38: Boolean = true

scala> employees.exists(x => x == doc2)
res39: Boolean = true

scala> employees.exists(x => x == engineers)
res40: Boolean = false

scala> emp2.exists(x => x == engineers)
res42: Boolean = true
```

In the code snippet above, we first created the abstract *Employee* class, which has common attributes. Then we created the case classes *Engineer* and *Doctor*, each extending the abstract class *Employee*. After that we created a couple of sample data for both types of employee. This is followed by creating a list for each category. Those two lists are then combined using two different methods—using the operator ::: and *List*. Note that one forms a list, while the other forms a list of lists. This affects searching. The one that forms a list of lists can identify the engineers' group as well as the doctors' group. The operator performs a flat combination and hence group information is no longer available.

Now, let's take another problem and develop an application using lists. Our task is to create a mini-dictionary containing at least the following words: apple, cow, color, god, goat, dog, house, mother, orange, rat, zeal, university. Here are the additional requirements:

1. Sort the words in ascending order.
2. Find whether there are duplicate words in the dictionary.
3. Find the total number of words in the dictionary.
4. Find whether the word "monkey" exists. Also check whether the word "university" exists.
5. Use immutable APIs as much as possible; however, you may use *println* for manual validation.

Figure 4.1 presents a typical solution for the mini-dictionary problem. First we create a list containing our vocabulary and then we print both the original version and the sorted version so that we can compare and validate the correctness of our program. Next, we calculate the total number of duplicate words. This is followed by the total number of words. In the last two LOCs, we check whether the given words "monkey" and "university" exist, respectively.

Exercise 4.1. *Word Count by Alphabet

The solution presented in Figure 4.1 gives the total count of words in a list. Write a program that outputs a count of words by alphabet. For example, if there are two words starting with the letter 'a', in the list, then the count for 'a' would be 2. What is the time complexity of your solution? Hint: In order to calculate time complexity, if you are using Scala collections, refer to the "Performance Characteristics" page of the Scala documentation [Col18].

```
package com.equalinformation.dascala.scala.lists

object MiniDictionaryApp {
    def main(args: Array[String]): Unit = {
        val myDict = List( "apple", "cow", "color", "god",
          "goat", "dog", "house", "mother", "orange",
          "rat", "zeal","university",
          "honorificabilitudinitatibus",
          "floccinaucinihilipilification",
          "pseudopseudohypoparathyroidism",
          "supercalifragilisticexpialidocious",
          "pneumonoultramicroscopicsilicovolcanoconiosis" )

        myDict.foreach(x => println(x))
        myDict.sorted.foreach(x => println(x))

        println("Total number of duplicate words: " +
           myDict.groupBy(identity).collect {
              case (x, List(_, _, _*)) => x
           }.size)

        println("Total number of words: "+myDict.size)
        println(myDict.exists(x => x == "monkey"))
        println(myDict.exists(x => x == "university"))
    }
}
```

Fig. 4.1: Mini dictionary

4.3 Analysis

We used Scala's existing libraries in order to implement our business problem. Also, the core operations are functional in nature. Sometimes, it is helpful to analyze what a functional structure translates to during compilation. Many functional structures are converted to loops, specially those that need to iterate over a collection.

For Scala's *List*, getting the head takes constant time, which is $O(1)$; also, getting the tail has the same time complexity. Prepending to a list also takes $O(1)$ time; however, appending to a list requires traversing all the way to the end of the list and hence requires $O(n)$ time. Similarly, *update* and *apply* have $O(n)$ time complexity. If we use *length* or *reverse* in our program then we are introducing $O(n)$ time complexity. Knowing the time complexity of built-in methods or functions is very helpful to come up with the overall time complexity of our programs. This also gives us an idea of when to develop our own libraries.

Google is one such company that develops its own libraries and frameworks when the available open source technology doesn't meet its performance requirements. The same is true with Apple, Amazon, Facebook, etc. So if you plan to apply for jobs in one of those companies or their competitors, it is certainly helpful to know the limitations of existing open source libraries and how to improve those or write new ones from scratch. This is one of the reasons why interviews in these companies emphasize heavily on data structures and algorithms, among other things.

If time permits, it is recommended to scan the source code of Scala's *List* implementation [Lis18]. We see that *List* is declared as an abstract class.

```
abstract class List[+A]
```

This means it cannot be instantiated. Also, we notice that it has a type parameter A, with + in front of it, which means lists are covariant. For example, if *Employee* is a super type of *Engineer*, then *List* < *Employee* > automatically becomes a super type of *List* < *Engineer* >. This allows us to assign a value of type *List* < *Engineer* > to a variable of type *List* < *Employee* >. We created such lists in Section 4.2.

4.4 Application

Both immutable and mutable versions of lists are used heavily in practice. If we have large code bases written in Java, we might find a mutable version of the list. If we are doing concurrent and distributed programming, it is good to start with the immutable version and then migrate to a mutable version if the context demands. It is much more complex to provide data consistency for mutable data in distributed and concurrent programming environments.

If we are doing functional programming, the chances are very high that we will be living and breathing lists. There are three basic operations—*head*, *tail*, *isEmpty*. Let's look at the the following code snippet as a reminder.

```
scala> val f1: (Int, Int) => Int = _ + _
f1: (Int, Int) => Int = <function2>

scala> val f2: (Int, Int) => Int = _ - _
f2: (Int, Int) => Int = <function2>

scala> val f3: (Int, Int) => Int = _ * _
f3: (Int, Int) => Int = <function2>

scala> val fnList = List(f1,f2,f3)
fnList: List[(Int, Int) => Int] = List(<function2>,
 <function2>, <function2>)

scala> fnList.head
res6: (Int, Int) => Int = <function2>

scala> fnList.tail
```

```
res7: List[(Int, Int) => Int] = List(<function2>,
 <function2>)

scala> val myNumbers = List(1,2,3,4,5)
myNumbers: List[Int] = List(1, 2, 3, 4, 5)

scala> myNumbers.isEmpty
res0: Boolean = false

scala> myNumbers.head
res1: Int = 1

scala> myNumbers.tail
res2: List[Int] = List(2, 3, 4, 5)
```

The operations look fairly simple; we can make a list of functions or a list of numbers or some other types. The operations *head*, *tail*, and *isEmpty* can be applied to any type of list, as shown above. Here, *List* provides us with the ability to house series of algorithms and apply those to some data.

In imperative programming, we deal a lot with loops, which are also known as control structures. Scala is an expression-oriented language that supports functional programming. Just to emphasize the application of lists, we have a historical programming language called LISP (LISt Processor), also referred as Lisp [McC60]. The original paper written by John McCarthy starts with "Recursive functions of symbolic expressions." We see that the focus is on functions and expressions and their computation by machine. Many functional languages were influenced by Lisp, as was Scala. Hence, lists are likely to appear in many functional data structure implementation tasks.

Exercise 4.2. *Application of $fold$, $foldLeft$, and $foldRight$ Functions*

Given the following signature for three implementations of folding—*fold*, *foldLeft*, and *foldRight*, write sample programs of your choice to demonstrate how these functions work. In your explanation, show detailed calculation steps for at least one application, demonstrating operations for all three functions.

```
def fold[A1 >: A](z: A1)(op: (A1, A1) => A1): A1
def foldLeft[B](z: B)(op: (B, A) => B): B
def foldRight[B](z: B)(op: (A, B) => B): B
```

Exercise 4.3. *Get, Average, and Reversal*

Given a list, perform the following:

1. Given an integer index, get the value corresponding to this index.
2. Calculate the average of values.
3. Reverse the list.
4. Get the last element using *foldLeft*.
5. Calculate the length using *foldLeft*.

Chapter 5
Stacks

We observe stacks of things in our daily life—stacks of books in a library, stacks of plates in a cafeteria, stacks of boxes in a store, etc. Even though these are different kinds of things, there are several commonalities, in terms of how items are taken out or put into these stacks. For example, whether it is a book or a plate, the one that is placed on the stack last is on top of the stack and it is the first one to be removed. So it is a *Last In First Out (LIFO)* stack.

In computer science, this structure is handy where we need to enforce the *LIFO* rule. For example, if we want to check whether opening parentheses match with closing parentheses in an expression, we can use a stack. Anywhere order checking is needed this structure is handy.

5.1 Structure

A stack can be treated as a container that has a single opening, i.e., items can be inserted and removed using that end only. Naturally, there are operations of interest:

- Insert an item.
- Remove an item.
- Check whether the stack is empty.
- Check whether the stack is full.

5.2 Typical Implementation

We present a typical implementation of a stack in Figure 5.1. The *MyStack* class has five operations. The first one, called *push*, accepts data of type *Double* and inserts it into the stack. When an item is pushed, *top* is increased by 1. Similarly, *pop* does the opposite of what *push* does, i.e., it removes an item from the stack and then

© Springer Nature Switzerland AG 2019
B. P. Upadhyaya, *Data Structures and Algorithms with Scala*, Undergraduate
Topics in Computer Science, https://doi.org/10.1007/978-3-030-12561-5_5

decreases *top* by 1. *peek* differs from *pop* in the sense that it returns the item on the top but doesn't remove the item. More accurately, it doesn't change the pointer to the top. *isEmpty* returns a *Boolean* value that tells whether the stack is empty. Similarly, *isFull* tells us whether the stack is full. Note that the stack implementation makes use of the *Array* data structure described in Chapter 3.

Now, on the main method side, we create a stack with capacity to hold eight elements. The type of these elements is fixed during the *stackBox* definition, which in this case is *Double*. Next, we insert elements into the stack and then remove them until the stack is empty. The whole implementation validates our stack explanation.

Exercise 5.1. *Functional Implementation*

Functional programming is being slowly adopted by the industry. Scala played an instrumental role by fusing object-oriented programming with functional programming. In this context, implement a functional stack. The one implemented in Figure 5.1 is an imperative implementation.

```scala
package com.equalinformation.dascala.scala.stacks

class MyStack(maxSize: Int) {
    private var stackBox = new Array[Double](maxSize)
    private var top = -1

    def push(data: Double): Unit = {
        top += 1
        stackBox(top) = data
    }

    def pop(): Double = {
        val popData = stackBox(top)
        top -= 1
        popData
    }

    def peek(): Double = {
        stackBox(top)
    }

    def isEmpty(): Boolean = {
        return (top == -1)
    }

    def isFull(): Boolean = {
        return (top == maxSize - 1)
    }
    }

object StackApp {
    def main(args: Array[String]): Unit = {
        val myStack = new MyStack(8)
        myStack.push(5)
        myStack.push(10)
        myStack.push(20)

        while(!myStack.isEmpty) {
            println(myStack.pop())
        }

    }
}
```

Fig. 5.1: A typical stack implementation

5.3 Analysis

A stack is a simple data structure that is handy for many operations requiring ordering or order enforcement. The space complexity for n *push* operations is $O(n)$ whereas it has an $O(1)$ average case. Similarly, *pop* and *peek* have $O(1)$ complexity, which is true for *isEmpty* and *isFull*.

5.4 Application

First, let's discuss one of the applications of stacks. The task, for us, is to reverse a given word. We present a complete solution in Figure 5.2. The class *MyStackChar* takes the maximum size of the stack as a constructor parameter, which is the length of the input. Next, we define all stack-related operations.

Then we have the *Reverser* class that contains the actual logic to reverse a given word. It takes the input word as its constructor parameter. We make use of *StringBuilder* so that we can use its *append* method to form the reversed word. The method *reverse* creates *myStack*, which is an instance of *MyStackChar*. Next, we push every character in the word to the stack. When the characters are pushed into the stack, the first character is at the bottom of the stack, the second character on top of it, and so on. In this way, the last character to be inserted is the last character of the word, which is popped first and appended to the collector *output*. The first character of the word is the last one to be popped and appended. This is how a given word is reversed using a stack structure.

We can solve this problem using a plain array. But the solution presented here is conceptually neat because the rules are clearer. Also, the solution presented in Figure 5.2 doesn't allow bugs to be introduced by custom handling of word indices. See the code snippet below: it is hard to introduce a bug unknowingly as indices are not directly present.

```
for(eachChar <- word) {
    myStack.push(eachChar)
}
```

The stack structure can be used to solve a wide variety of problems. For example, it can be used to match HTML and XML tags. Another common problem in computer science is converting infix notations to postfix notations. Also it can be used to evaluate expressions, for example, postfix operations. Internally, it can be used to compute recursive structures and other function calls.

```scala
package com.equalinformation.dascala.scala.stacks

class MyStackChar(maxSize: Int) {
   private var stackBox = new Array[Char](maxSize)
   private var top = -1

   def push(data: Char): Unit = {
      top += 1
      stackBox(top) = data
   }

   def pop(): Char = {
      val popData = stackBox(top)
      top -= 1
      popData
   }

   def peek(): Char = {
      stackBox(top)
   }

   def isEmpty(): Boolean = {
      return (top == -1)
   }

   def isFull(): Boolean = {
      return (top == maxSize - 1)
   }
}

class Reverser(word: String) {
   private val output: StringBuilder = new StringBuilder

   def reverse(): StringBuilder = {
      val myStack = new MyStackChar(word.length)

      for(eachChar <- word) {
         myStack.push(eachChar)
      }

      while(!myStack.isEmpty) {
         val poppedChar: Char = myStack.pop
         output.append(poppedChar)
      }

      output
   }
}

object WordReverseApp {
   def main(args: Array[String]): Unit = {
      print("Enter a word: ")
      val inputWord = scala.io.StdIn.readLine().toString
      val myReverser = new Reverser(inputWord)

      println("Reverse word: " + myReverser.reverse)
   }
}
```

Fig. 5.2: Word reversing

Exercise 5.2. *Stack Implementation Enhancement*

Enhance the implementation of *MyStackChar* in Figure 5.2 so that we don't need
multiple stack classes defined. For your testing you can use the existing *Reverser*
class and *WordReverseApp*. Since *Reverser* is in the same package, you don't have
to import it. The object *WordReverseApp* might need renaming if you create a textual copy, as the Scala compiler will complain about duplicate objects.

Chapter 6
Queues

Queues are common in the real world. For example, we stand in a queue when we go to a cafeteria; there are queues in restaurants, at ticket counters, at airport check-in desks, etc. All of these queues have common rules. These rules are defined by the owner of the queues. Interestingly, the queues in the cafeteria at Apple operate the same way as the queues in Google's cafeteria. As of 2018, Google's cafeteria offers free food whereas Apple's cafeteria needs payment. In spite of this difference, the queue rules are the same. Normally, we don't find a handbook that tells how queues should operate in both of these companies, but still they operate uniformly. Why?

Similarly, in computer science we have uniformity in the structure of certain things. In operating systems there are many processes requiring resources. These processes can be put in a queue and then allocated resources based on their arrival priority. Sometimes, it might be necessary to assign priority to certain types of processes. In such cases, we have new rules for operation, i.e., the items with higher priority come out of the queue first. This type of structure is known as a priority queue.

6.1 Structure

A queue, in general, can be thought of a pipe that is open at both ends so that items enter from one end and exit from the other. In computer science, a queue can be thought of as a container where items can be inserted and removed based on their arrival order. This kind of structure defines a set of rules:

- An item that is inserted first is the first one to be removed. There is a popular acronym for this: *First in First Out (FIFO)*.
- An item that is inserted last leaves the queue last.
- Processes serving a queue often check whether the queue is full or empty.
- There should be a way to insert and remove an item from the queue.

© Springer Nature Switzerland AG 2019
B. P. Upadhyaya, *Data Structures and Algorithms with Scala*, Undergraduate
Topics in Computer Science, https://doi.org/10.1007/978-3-030-12561-5_6

6.2 Typical Implementation

In Figure 6.1, we present a typical implementation of a queue. The class *MyQueue* takes the maximum size of the queue as a constructor parameter. Then, based on the parameterized maximum size, we create *queueBox*, with the help of array data structure. When the queue is empty, the front index is 0, and we set *rear* to -1. Similarly, the maximum number of items in the queue is also 0.

Next we define the *insert* method, which accepts data of any type. In its body, first, we check the value of *rear*: if it is *maxSize* − 1, then we reset it, since it has reached the full capacity of the queue. Next, we increase the value of *rear* by 1, and data is inserted using *rear* as an index. Accordingly, the number of items in the queue is increased.

When we remove an item from the queue, we return that item. In the body of the method *remove*, we get the item at index *front* and assign it to a temporary holder *tempData*. Then the value of *front* is increased by 1. If *front* reaches the maximum value for this queue, we reset it. When we remove an item, the number of items in the queue decreases by 1.

The method *peekFront* returns the item at the front of the queue but doesn't change the indexing. Indices change only when items are inserted or removed. *isEmpty* checks whether the queue is empty or not and *isFull*, as the name suggests, returns true if the queue is full; otherwise it returns false.

Once the queue definition is complete, we write the *main* method. First, we create an instance of *MyQueue*, with capacity 10. Then we insert three elements. In order to verify our implementation, we remove elements one by one until the queue is empty. If the queue is correctly implemented then the item inserted first should be printed first. This completes our queue implementation.

Exercise 6.1. *Queue Implementation Improvement*

The implementation in Figure 6.1 might face performance issues when there are large numbers of insertions and deletions. Find a typical number when performance starts degrading. Then suggest improvements and implement those suggestions. There is at least one bug in the program: identify the bug and implement your fix.

Now, let's looks at the application presented in Figure 6.2. This is a typical functional implementation of queue. First we define a case class *FQueue*, which has two constructor parameters—*out* and *in*. As mentioned in Chapter 4, lists are the fundamental structures in functional programming, as arrays are for imperative programming.

The case class has a method *check* to check the invariant, i.e., it should always be possible to extract an element from a non-empty list. Next, we define the application object *FunctQueueApp* and house necessary methods there. Unlike the case of

```scala
package com.equalinformation.dascala.scala.queues

class MyQueue(maxSize: Int) {
    private var queueBox: Array[Any] = new Array[Any](maxSize)
    private var front: Int = 0
    private var rear: Int = -1
    private var numOfItems: Int = 0

    def insert(data: Any): Unit = {
        if(rear == maxSize - 1) {
            rear = -1
        }

        rear += 1
        queueBox(rear) = data
        numOfItems += 1
    }

    def remove(): Any = {
        val tempData: Any = queueBox(front)
        front += 1

        if(front == maxSize) {
            front = 0
        }

        numOfItems -= 1
        tempData
    }

    def peekFront(): Any = {
        queueBox(front)
    }

    def isEmpty(): Boolean = {
        numOfItems == 0
    }

    def isFull(): Boolean = {
        numOfItems == maxSize
    }

}

object QueueApp {
    def main(args: Array[String]): Unit = {
        val myQueue = new MyQueue(10)

        myQueue.insert(5)
        myQueue.insert(10)
        myQueue.insert(15)

        while(!myQueue.isEmpty()) {
            println(myQueue.remove())
        }

    }
}
```

Fig. 6.1: A typical queue implementation

imperative programming, here we define queue operations in the application class itself. This comes from the idea of functional composition. Let's discuss the *insert* and *remove* methods first. The *out* field can be *Nil* if *in* is *Nil*. Otherwise, the new *in* gets a value which is the concatenation of the data element with the old *in*.

Now, let's analyze the *remove* method. It takes a queue and returns an integer value and a queue. The integer value is the head and the returned queue is the tail of the input queue. In order for the output to be *Nil*, the queue should be empty.

Next, in the main, we create *myQueue* by inserting elements. Note the order: the innermost element is the first one to be inserted and hence is the first to be removed from the queue. In order to verify this, we apply *remove* once and print so that we can visually check whether right element is coming out of the queue. The output should look like the following:

```
(5,FQueue(List(10, 15),List()))
```

The *insert* method takes a data element and a queue as its inputs and returns a queue as its output. The new input is formed by concatenating the data element with the *in* field of *queue*.

Exercise 6.2. *Functional Queue*

For the implementation in Figure 6.2, perform the following:

1. Modify the program so that multiple types can be used during testing.
2. Make the necessary modification to extract the value enqueued in the second position.

```
package com.equalinformation.dascala.scala.queues

case class FQueue(out: List[Int], in: List[Int]) {
   def check(): Boolean = (out, in) match {
      case (Nil, x :: xs) => false
      case _ => true
   }

   require(check, "Didn't satisfy invariant")
}

object FunctQueueApp {
   def main(args: Array[String]): Unit = {
      val myQueue = insert(15, insert(10, insert(5,
         FQueue(Nil, Nil))))
      println(remove(myQueue))
   }

   def insert(data: Int, queue: FQueue): FQueue = {
      val newIn = data :: queue.in
      queue.out match {
         case Nil => FQueue(newIn.reverse, Nil)
         case _ => queue.copy(in = newIn)
      }
   }

   def remove(queue: FQueue): (Int, FQueue) = {
      queue.out match {
         case Nil => throw new
            IllegalArgumentException("Queue is empty!")
         case x :: Nil => (x, queue.copy(out =
            queue.in.reverse, Nil))
         case y :: ys => (y, queue.copy(out = ys))
      }
   }

}
```

Fig. 6.2: A typical queue implementation – object-functional approach

6.3 Analysis

We have seen two implementations of the queue data structure, one in Figure 6.1 and the other one in Figure 6.2. The object-oriented implementation houses the queue operations in the object representing the queue, which is a typical way of writing object-oriented programs. Class attributes and operations are inside the class, and the software class represents a corresponding real-world class or object.

In object-functional implementation there is a mixed representation. We have a case class that can be used for pattern matching, one of the popular features of functional programming. When we have a class and an object, we could claim that the implementation is a sort of object-oriented programming, which is true, because Scala fuses two programming paradigms—object-oriented and functional. In an object-functional implementation, the core operations of a queue are housed in the application itself. It is more inclined toward developing applications by composing functions.

The time complexity of inserting and removing an item into the queue is $O(1)$.

6.4 Application

Queues are widely used in many applications of computer science. For example, queues are used in asynchronous data transfer, such as file IO. Files or chunks can be put in a queue based on the order of arrival. The destination can consume when it is ready and the queue guarantees the correct ordering. Similarly, queues can also be used to schedule jobs by an operating system, specially those jobs that have equal priority. Even though they have equal priority, they arrive at different times, and the queue uses timing to set their priorities. Last but not least, queues are used to implement other data structures and to solve algorithmic problems.

Queues can also be used effectively to solve many real-world problems. For example, queues at counters could be represented by software queues. With visual aids the servers can efficiently track and serve people in the queues. This also allows proper allocation of servers. Similarly, a suitable number of cashiers can be arranged in supermarkets based on queue size. Another application is to queue customers in call centers. Generally, these operate on a first come, first served basis, so queues are a natural representation. If we have preferred customers calling, they can be handled using priority queues.

Chapter 7
Hash Tables

In the real world we have large ranges. For example, positive integers can be close to infinity. A national identification number, like a social security number, can be a nine-digit number. We may not necessarily have that much space available, or in some cases it may not be efficient to allocate that much memory for the purpose of computation. In such scenarios, it is efficient to map these large ranges to smaller ranges that can be accommodated in computer memory. A data structure that makes use of this technique is called a hash table; it stores keys and their values and uses a *hash function* to map keys with their values. A hash table is one of the most efficient data structures, with running time $O(1)$ for search, insertion, and deletion. In the worst-case scenario, specially when linked lists are stored as values, the running time can be $O(n)$.

7.1 Structure and Algorithm

In terms of structure, a hash table is more like an array; however, the way elements are addressed is different. In an array, elements are addressed using direct addressing. In direct addressing, an element at position k is accessed using the index value k. In hash tables, keys are computed using a hash function. The core of a hash table lies in the ability to design a hash function that does efficient mapping between the real-world range or problem range and the range available (or allocated) in the computer. A good hash function can distribute real-world keys uniformly in the computer's memory without any collision. A collision occurs when two or more real-world keys are mapped to a single hash table key.

When the problem space keys have a very large range, it may not be possible to have unique corresponding keys in the hash table. In such scenarios, linked lists are used to provide additional identity. In addition to the key, object values can be compared. In such implementations, in the worst-case scenario it can take $O(n)$ time to find an element in the hash table. This is primarily because linked lists are involved.

© Springer Nature Switzerland AG 2019
B. P. Upadhyaya, *Data Structures and Algorithms with Scala*, Undergraduate
Topics in Computer Science, https://doi.org/10.1007/978-3-030-12561-5_7

A quick search in the ACM Digital Library or the IEEE Xplore Digital Library results in many research papers related to hash functions. It is not in the scope of this book to deal with hash function design in detail. This book, primarily, aims to provide good hands-on examples, from a coding perspective, specially functional implementations using Scala. However, we discuss a couple of techniques to design a hash function so that Scala coding makes better sense.

The first technique is simple. It is known as the *remainder method*. In this method, the hash code is calculated by dividing the key by the available array size. The remainder is the key value to be used in the hash table. For example, let's say there are 1000 keys in the problem space and we have available array size of 17. Now, a hash key for a randomly picked value between 0 and 1000 is calculated as: $hash(n) = n \% 17$. For example, the hash value for 35 is $hash(35) = 35 \% 17 = 1$. Similarly, the hash value for 999 = $hash(999) = 999 \% 17 = 13$. You may have already realized that there is a good chance of key collision.

A somewhat better hash function can be designed using the *multiplication method*. In this method, the hash function is defined as: $hash(key) = \lfloor m * ((key * R) \% 1) \rfloor$, where $0 < R < 1$. Let's pick $R = 0.201$. Now, $hash(35) = \lfloor 17 * ((35 * 0.201) \% 1) \rfloor = 2$. Calculating for 999: $hash(999) = \lfloor 17 * ((999 * 0.201) \% 1) \rfloor = 14$. It is apparent that the hash values differ. It should be fun to vary the array size and R and see how uniquely the hash table keys are generated for a given range of problem space keys. You are strongly encouraged to come up with your own hash function.

Exercise 7.1. *Dynamic Hash Functions*

Is it practical to create dynamic hash functions based on the available memory of a machine where a program or an application is running? If yes, make practical assumptions to design (or generate) dynamic hash functions. If no, provide your reasoning.

7.2 Typical Implementation

In this section, we present two versions of hash table implementation—mutable and immutable. Let's start with the mutable version. We present a mutable hash table implementation in Figure 7.1. The class *HashTableMutableImpl* has two parameterized types—*Key* and *Value*. Also, the class takes *size* as a constructor parameter, which is of type *Int*. It extends the mutable trait *HashTable*; since they are in the same package there is no need to explicitly import the trait. Next, we define a container called *myHashArray* that holds lists of keys and values. This is initialized with empty lists; the size of the array is defined by the constructor parameter *size*.

Next, we define a *hashCode* method, which calculates a hash code for a given key. The *Key* type is parameterized so that different types can be used. Scala provides the ## operation to calculate hash codes. We make use of this operation to calculate the hash code for our keys. We use the *remainder method* discussed in Section 7.1. If the calculated value is negative, we add the *size* value to it so that it becomes positive; otherwise we return as it is.

Now, let's discuss the *insert* operation. This takes a key and value pair as its parameters and returns *Unit* type, which is equivalent to *void*. Since it changes the content of *myHashArray*, it doesn't have to return anything. We extract a list using a hash key obtained from *hashCode*. Next, we prepend the key-value pair to this list, making sure that there is no key matching the current key, which guarantees uniqueness. Then we assign this newly formed list to the same position in *myHashArray* from where the list was obtained. Basically, we have added a key-value pair to this list and placed it back in the array, in the same position; the position is determined by the hash code, which is calculated by the *hashCode* method using the incoming key.

Now, let's discuss the *search* operation. This takes a key and returns an *Option*. First we extract the corresponding list based on the hash key of the incoming key. Next, we find a pair so that the first element of the pair matches the incoming key and we return the second element of that matching pair, because the second element is the value that the *search* user is interested in.

Finally, we have the *delete* operation, which takes a key as its input parameter and returns an *Option*; this option contains the value that we deleted. In this method, first we extract the corresponding list using the hash key, which is based on the incoming key. Next, we filter a pair whose first element is equal to the incoming key; in another words, we logically remove the pair matching its key with the incoming key. The remaining contents of the list are assigned back to the same position in *myHashArray*. This does the delete operation. Lastly, we return the value of the pair whose key matches the incoming key.

Now it is time to test our mutable hash table implementation. We present the test application in Figure 7.2. First we have trait definition, which is obvious, because we already discussed its implementation. In the *main* method, we first create an instance of *HashTableMutableImpl*; the size is specified as 17. This value is used to calculate the hash key every time the *hashCode* method is invoked in *HashTableMutableImpl*. Then we insert five key-value pairs. The keys are similar to US social security numbers, without dashes. Next, we print the search results. Once successfully inserted, we should get *Some(< value >)* printed on the console. Next, we delete the "Ritchie" entry, which should be successfully deleted. In the last LOC, we search for the already deleted key, which maps to "Richie". So it should print *None* on the console. The second last LOC tries to delete the non-existing record, so it should print *None*. See the entire output below. This completes our discussion of mutable hash table implementation. Next, we will discuss the immutable version.

```
Martin search, Some(Martin)
James search, Some(James)
Brian search, Some(Brian)
Einstein search Some(Einstein)
```

```scala
package com.equalinformation.dascala.scala.hash_tables.mutable

class HashTableMutableImpl[Key, Value](size: Int) extends
  HashTable[Key, Value] {
    private val myHashArray = Array.fill(size)(List[(Key,
      Value)]())

    def hashCode[Key](myKey: Key) = {
        val tempHashCode = myKey.## % size
        if(tempHashCode < 0) tempHashCode + size else
          tempHashCode
    }

    override def insert(myKey: Key, myValue: Value): Unit = {
        val myList = myHashArray(hashCode(myKey))
        myHashArray(hashCode(myKey)) = (myKey, myValue) +:
          myList.filter(x => x._1 != myKey)
    }

    override def search(myKey: Key): Option[Value] = {
        val myList = myHashArray(hashCode(myKey))
        myList.find(x => x._1 == myKey).map(y => y._2)
    }

    override def delete(myKey: Key): Option[Value] = {
        val myList = myHashArray(hashCode(myKey))
        myHashArray(hashCode(myKey)) = myList.filter(x =>
          x._1 != myKey)
        myList.find(x => x._1 == myKey).map(y => y._2)
    }
}
```

Fig. 7.1: A typical mutable hash table implementation

```
Richie search, Some(Richie)
Richie delete, Some(Richie)
Non-existing delete, None
Richie search, None
```

In Figure 7.3, we present an immutable hash table implementation. Let's first discuss the corresponding immutable trait *HashTable*, which is presented in Figure 7.4:

```scala
trait HashTable[Key, Value] {
def insert(myKey: Key, myValue: Value):
HashTable[Key, Value]
def search(myKey: Key): Option[Value]
def delete(myKey: Key): HashTable[Key, Value]
}
```

```scala
package com.equalinformation.dascala.scala.hash_tables.mutable

trait HashTable[Key, Value] {
    def insert(myKey: Key, myValue: Value)
    def search(myKey: Key): Option[Value]
    def delete(myKey: Key): Option[Value]
}

object HashTableMutableApp {
    def main(args: Array[String]): Unit = {
        val myHashTable: HashTable[Int, String] =
          new HashTableMutableImpl[Int, String](17)

        myHashTable.insert(123456789, "Martin")
        myHashTable.insert(987654321, "James")
        myHashTable.insert(123454321, "Brian")
        myHashTable.insert(432112345, "Einstein")
        myHashTable.insert(776612345, "Richie")

        println(s" Martin search, ${myHashTable
          .search(123456789)}")
        println(s"James search, ${myHashTable
          .search(987654321)}")
        println(s"Brian search, ${myHashTable
          .search(123454321)}")
        println(s"Einstein search ${myHashTable
          .search(432112345)}")
        println(s"Richie search, ${myHashTable
          .search(776612345)}")

        println(s"Richie delete, ${myHashTable
          .delete(776612345)}")
        println(s"Non-existing delete, ${myHashTable
          .delete(886612345)}")
        println(s"Richie search, ${myHashTable
          .search(776612345)}")
    }
}
```

Fig. 7.2: Mutable hash table test application

Unlike the mutable version, the immutable *insert* has to return a new *HashTable*, as it doesn't modify the existing hash table. It copies the existing hash table instead of modifying it; this is how immutable operations work. Similarly, the *delete* operation returns a new *HashTable*, which is one element less than the original copy for a successful delete; the original copy remains as it is. The *search* operation is the same as that of the mutable version, as neither version has to modify anything. They just read a record. If a record exists for a given key then it returns *Some(< value >)*; otherwise *None*.

Now, let's discuss the *HashTableImmutableImpl* class. This is a protected class and is not meant to be accessed from outside. So the test application calls the singleton object, which has the *apply* method in it serving as a factory method. This method has the *size* parameter, which can be passed while calling this object. Internally the singleton object creates a vector of specified size and fills it with empty lists. Also, it creates an instance of the *HashTableImmutableImpl* class by passing the vector *myHashVector*. We use *Vector* for the immutable implementation because it provides a similar structure to that of the *Array* and has a *Trie* structure implemented underneath. This improves the performance of the immutable implementation; however, the performance may not be as good as that of a mutable implementation.

In *HashTableImmutableImpl*, *size* is calculated based on the size of *myHashVector*; this size is used to calculate the hash code for a given key. The method *hashCode* is the same as that of the mutable version. The *insert* method signature doesn't explicitly specify return type, which is implicit in this case. First we calculate the insertion index using the incoming key. Then we get the corresponding list from *myHashVector*. We create a new list by prepending the incoming key-value pair to this list. As in the mutable version, we make sure the incoming key is unique by applying *filter*. Next, a new instance of *HashTableImmutableImpl* is created, which has updated *myHashVector*; the position *insertionIndex* is updated by *newList*.

The *search* method is the same as that of the mutable version. First, we get a list corresponding to the hash key generated using the incoming key. Then we find a key-value pair whose key matches the incoming key and then return the second element of the pair, which is the value for a given key.

Finally, the *delete* method performs the removal operation. Like the *insert* method, it has an implicit return type, which is comes from Scala's type inference. First, we calculate the deletion index based on the incoming key. Then we get a list corresponding to this index. In order to perform deletion, we retain records that do not match the incoming key; in other words, records whose keys match the incoming key are filtered out. The filtered list is then assigned to a new *val*, which then updates the *deletionIndex*. A new *HashTableImmutableImpl* is returned.

Now, let's test our immutable hash map implementation. We present the test application in Figure 7.4. We have already discussed the immutable trait *HashTable*, which is not part of the test application but is placed here for convenience. In the *main* method, first, we get an instance of *HashTableImmutableImpl* class. Note that we do not explicitly create an instance here; rather we get an instance by calling the *apply* method of the singleton object *HashTableImmutableImpl*. We pass the size value as 17. Next, we insert all the records. Note that we do insertion in a single statement; basically insert a new key-value pair into the result of the previous insertion. If we do the same as in mutable version we end up with five *val* identifiers, because each insertion returns a new *HashTable*.

Next, we print the result of the *search* operation. All of these statements should print *Some(< value >)* if the corresponding key-value pairs have been successfully inserted. Then we remove a key-value pair corresponding to "Richie". Note that we assign it to a variable because we get a new *HashTable*; we need to use

```scala
package com.equalinformation.dascala.scala
  .hash_tables.immutable

protected class HashTableImmutableImpl[Key, Value](
  myHashVector: Vector[List[(Key, Value)]]) extends
  HashTable[Key, Value] {

  private val size = myHashVector.size

  def hashCode[Key](myKey: Key) = {
    val tempHashCode = myKey.## % size
    if(tempHashCode < 0) tempHashCode + size else
      tempHashCode
  }

  override def insert(myKey: Key, myValue: Value) = {
    val insertionIndex = hashCode(myKey)
    val insertionList = myHashVector(insertionIndex)
    val newList = (myKey, myValue) +: insertionList
      .filter(_._1 != myKey)

    new HashTableImmutableImpl[Key, Value](myHashVector
      .updated(insertionIndex, newList))
  }

  override def search(myKey: Key): Option[Value] = {
    val myList = myHashVector(hashCode(myKey))
    myList.find(x => x._1 == myKey).map(y => y._2)
  }

  override def delete(myKey: Key) = {
    val deletionIndex = hashCode(myKey)
    val deletionList = myHashVector(deletionIndex)
    val newList = deletionList.filter(_._1 != myKey)

    new HashTableImmutableImpl[Key, Value](myHashVector
      .updated(deletionIndex, newList))
  }
}

object HashTableImmutableImpl {
  def apply[Key, Value](size: Int) = {
    val myHashVector = Vector.fill(size)(List())

    new HashTableImmutableImpl[Key, Value](myHashVector)
  }
}
```

Fig. 7.3: A typical immutable hash table implementation

this hash table if we want to test whether our deletion was successful. Similarly, we try to delete a non-existing value as well. Next, we search for the "Richie" record in *removedRichie*, which should return *None*, as is the case for a non-existing record in *nonExisting*. Finally, we search for the "Richie" record in *filledTable*, which is unmodified by the delete operation as it is immutable. So it should return *Some(Richie)*. Below, we list the complete output of this test program. This completes our discussion of immutable hash table implementation.

```
Martin search, Some(Martin)
James search, Some(James)
Brian search, Some(Brian)
Einstein search Some(Einstein)
Richie search, Some(Richie)
Richie search, None
Non-existing search, None
Richie search in original, Some(Richie)
```

Exercise 7.2. *Mutable Vs. Immutable Hash Table*

Create the necessary test data to test both the mutable as well as immutable implementation of hash table presented in this chapter. Based on your test results, discuss which one is more efficient. Hint: you may need a substantially large data set or its equivalent in order to find a performance difference.

```scala
package com.equalinformation.dascala.scala
  .hash_tables.immutable

trait HashTable[Key, Value] {
   def insert(myKey: Key, myValue: Value):
     HashTable[Key, Value]
   def search(myKey: Key): Option[Value]
   def delete(myKey: Key): HashTable[Key, Value]
}

object HashTableImmutableApp {
   def main(args: Array[String]): Unit = {
      val myHashTable: HashTable[Int, String] =
        HashTableImmutableImpl(17)

      val filledTable = myHashTable.insert(123456789, "Martin")
        .insert(987654321, "James")
        .insert(123454321, "Brian")
        .insert(432112345, "Einstein")
        .insert(776612345, "Richie")

      println(s" Martin search, ${filledTable
        .search(123456789)}")
      println(s"James search, ${filledTable
        .search(987654321)}")
      println(s"Brian search, ${filledTable
        .search(123454321)}")
      println(s"Einstein search ${filledTable
        .search(432112345)}")
      println(s"Richie search, ${filledTable
        .search(776612345)}")

      val removedRichie = filledTable.delete(776612345)
      val nonExisting = filledTable.delete(886612345)

      println(s"Richie search, ${removedRichie
        .search(776612345)}")
      println(s"Non-existing search, ${nonExisting
        .search(886612345)}")
      println(s"Richie search in original, ${filledTable
        .search(776612345)}")
   }
}
```

Fig. 7.4: Immutable hash table test application

7.3 Analysis

In Section 7.2, we presented implementations of both mutable and immutable versions of a hash table. Ideally a hash table has running time complexity of $O(1)$ for insert, search, and delete operations. This can change when a linked list is used to handle collision. In this case, the best running time is $O(1)$. If we have to traverse to the end of a linked list then the running time complexity is $O(m)$, where m is the number of elements in the corresponding linked list.

The mutable version of our implementation is more efficient than the immutable version. But the immutable version is better suited for concurrency, as it doesn't modify the original hash table; it creates a new copy and makes modifications to that copy. That's why immutable hash tables are called persistent hash tables. The advantage is that we don't lose the original data copy so we can easily recover any inconsistent state. The disadvantage is that there are multiple copies. If the data to be handled is very large, this process is certainly going to occupy more memory. Since computer memory is not infinite, we need to find better way of handling it. That is why we used *Vector* to implement immutable hash tables. *Vector*, internally, implements a *Trie* data structure, which eliminates some of the duplications.

7.4 Application

Hash tables come in handy every time we encounter problems that require us to map keys with values in constant time for lookup, add, and remove. Since a hash table is one of the fastest performing data structures, often programmers look for an opportunity to transform other data structures into hash tables whenever there is an opportunity. If we are going through a typical Scala or Java workspace for a real-world application, we are very likely to find some use of a hash table.

Dictionaries and *HashMap* are applications of hash tables. Similarly, if we look at file systems, we have name and path and physical location to track, among other items. Paths and physical locations are stored as an application of a hash table. Another interesting application of hash functions is password verification. A highly secure web application doesn't send your password to the server side for verification, because that password can be intercepted en route. Instead, the application generates a hash code based on your password using special cryptographic hash functions. These cryptographic functions are sophisticated enough that it is very hard to generate a hash code equivalent to the hash code generated by the application for your password. On the server side, the transmitted hash code is compared with the stored hash code for your password. This means double security: even if the hash code storage system is compromised, it is still very hard to know your password, because the hash code of your password is stored, not your password. Another application of hashing is cloud storage, such as Google Drive and Dropbox. In these systems, hashing is used to optimize storage and search.

Chapter 8
Binary Trees

Hierarchical structures are abundant the nature. For example, a family tree helps us to understand relationships. It is a most talked about topic. We are interested to know where we lie in terms of the whole family structure, and that helps us to discover our new relatives. An academic ancestry tree shows how a particular school of thought has propagated over a period of time.

One of the advantages of tree representation of information is the convenience of analysis. When we put information in a tree structure certain relationships can be seen much more quickly compared to any textual representation. Also trees have certain properties, which we will explore in detail in this chapter, that allow us to do efficient information synthesis.

In the world of computer science, a tree is a nonlinear data structure that models hierarchical structures. These hierarchical structures may come from the real world or from human-made systems. A *binary tree* is a special form of tree, i.e., it has at most two children. Information represented in the form of binary trees is a lot more convenient to process, as binary trees show certain properties. For example, if we have two children they are easy to manage, but that may not be true when we have many more children. There will be a lot to track and take care of.

8.1 Structure and Algorithms

Formally, a binary tree can be represented with a triple, $T = (x, L, R)$, where x represents a node and L and R represent a left branch and a right branch, respectively. Also L and R are disjoint binary trees and do not contain x. The term binary comes from there being two children, i.e., every node in a binary tree can have at most two children. Also this is referred as the *degree* of a binary tree, which is 2. For a binary tree to be a full or complete binary tree it has to satisfy two conditions:

1. All of its leaves are at the same level and
2. Every interior node has two children.

© Springer Nature Switzerland AG 2019
B. P. Upadhyaya, *Data Structures and Algorithms with Scala*, Undergraduate Topics in Computer Science, https://doi.org/10.1007/978-3-030-12561-5_8

Here are some important definitions related to the structure of binary trees, or trees in general.

- *path*: This is defined as a sequence of nodes $(x_0, x_1, x_2, ..., x_n)$, where nodes with adjacent subscripts are adjacent nodes. Since trees are acyclic, a path cannot contain the same node more than once.
- *path length*: This is defined as the number n of its adjacent pairs.
- *root path*: For a node x_0, its root path is defined as a path $(x_0, x_1, x_2, ..., x_n)$, where x_n is the root of a tree.
- *depth*: This is defined as the length of its root path.
- *height*: This is defined as the greatest depth among all of its nodes
- *level*: This is the set of all nodes at a given depth.
- *size*: This is defined as the number of non-leaf nodes.

Now, let's look at tree traversal algorithms.

8.1.1 Preorder

1. Visit the root.
2. Perform a preorder traversal on the left subtree if it is nonempty.
3. Perform a preorder traversal on the right subtree if it is nonempty.

8.1.2 Inorder

1. Perform an inorder traversal on the left subtree if it is nonempty.
2. Visit the root.
3. Perform an inorder traversal on the right subtree if it is nonempty.

8.1.3 Postorder

1. Perform a postorder traversal on the left subtree if it is nonempty.
2. Perform a postorder traversal on the right subtree if it is nonempty.
3. Visit the root.

8.2 Typical Implementation

In Figure 8.1, we present a typical implementation of a binary tree. Now, let's analyze the code. We define a generic type-based binary tree using:

```
sealed trait BinaryTree[+A]
```

This is sealed and the type is covariant. Since it is sealed, it can only be extended in the same source file, which helps the compiler to check for exhaustive pattern matching.

Next, we have a case object called *Leaf*, which is a binary tree of *Nothing* as it doesn't have any value and subtrees.

```
case object Leaf extends BinaryTree[Nothing]
```

We need one more component to create a binary tree, i.e., a construct that helps us to create branches. Since we use pattern matching extensively in order to process binary trees, this is also going to be a case class, as shown in the code snippet below.

```
case class Branch[A](value: A, left: BinaryTree[A],
    right: BinaryTree[A]) extends BinaryTree[A]
```

A branch node has a value of type *A* and two subtrees—a left subtree and a right subtree. We can see that it is recursive structure, which is one of the reasons for the code being succinct.

The method *createTree*, in Figure 8.1, takes a list and creates a binary tree out of this list. If the list is empty that matches the *Leaf* case, i.e., we return *Leaf*. When the list has one or more elements we build a tree. Half of the elements are used to create a left subtree and the other half for a right subtree.

In order to calculate the size of a binary tree, we define the *size* method. If a tree is a *Leaf* node, then the size is 0. Otherwise, we compute the size recursively at each node. The size of the tree at a node is calculated by adding the accumulated sum increased by 1 (the size of the current node), the size of the left subtree, and the size of the right subtree. This is captured by the expression:

```
1 + size(leftBranch) + size(rightBranch)
```

Similarly, we use a recursive structure to calculate the depth of a binary tree, as shown in Figure 8.1. For a tree that has only a leaf, the depth is 0. Otherwise, the depth at each node is calculated as a sum of the accumulated sum increased by 1 (the depth of the current node) and the maximum depth of subtrees. If the left tree is deeper than the right subtree then the depth of the left subtree is considered for calculation and vice versa.

Exercise 8.1. *Binary Tree Equality*

Write an application to check whether two given binary trees are equal. It is recommended to use recursive structures for your implementation for brevity.

```
package com.equalinformation.dascala.scala.bin_trees

sealed trait BinaryTree[+A]
case object Leaf extends BinaryTree[Nothing]
case class Branch[A](value: A, left: BinaryTree[A],
  right: BinaryTree[A]) extends BinaryTree[A]

object BinaryTreeApp {
  def main(args: Array[String]): Unit = {
    val myList = List(1,2,3,4,5,6)
    val myBinTree = createTree(myList)
    println(myBinTree)
    println(size(myBinTree))
    println(depth(myBinTree))
  }

  def createTree[A](list: List[A]): BinaryTree[A] =
    list match {
      case Nil => Leaf
      case x :: xs => {
      val halfLength = xs.length / 2
      Branch(x, createTree(xs.take(halfLength)),
        createTree(xs.drop(halfLength)))
      }
    }

  def size[A](binTree: BinaryTree[A]): Int = binTree match {
    case Leaf => 0
    case Branch(_, leftBranch, rightBranch) => 1 +
      size(leftBranch) + size(rightBranch)
  }

  def depth[A](binTree: BinaryTree[A]): Int = binTree match {
    case Leaf => 0
    case Branch(_, leftBranch, rightBranch) => 1 +
      (depth(leftBranch) max depth(rightBranch))
  }

}
```

Fig. 8.1: A typical binary tree implementation

Exercise 8.2. *Complete Binary Tree*

Using recursive structures, implement a complete binary tree.

Exercise 8.3. *Binary Tree Flipping*

Write an application to flip a binary tree.

Exercise 8.4. *Binary Tree Flipped Equality*

Write an application to check whether a binary tree is a flipped version of another binary tree.

Now, let's look at binary tree traversal algorithms. We present a complete solution in Figure 8.2. The method *preorder* takes a binary tree and returns a list of items from preorder traversal. If the tree has only one leaf then it returns *Nil* because there is no value present. For a non-empty tree, we apply a recursive structure to traverse the tree. We prepend the node value with the combined list of left subtree preorder traversal and right subtree preorder traversal.

Similarly, the method *inorder* takes a binary tree and returns a list that is the result of inorder traversal. If a tree has only a leaf, the ouput is *Nil*. Otherwise, the output is a combination of three items—the list obtained by performing inorder traversal on the left subtree, the node value, and the list obtained by performing inorder traversal on the right subtree. Note how operators apply to a list and a single value.

Next, the method *postorder* takes a tree and returns a list that is the result of postorder traversal. As for other traversals, if the tree contains only a leaf then the result is *Nil*. For a non-empty tree, we apply a recursive structure. In order to achieve postorder traversal, we first traverse the left subtree, get a list, and then join that list with the result of traversing the right subtree in postorder. Finally we join the node value.

In the *main* method, first we create a list, *myList*, containing six integer values, then we build a binary tree by invoking the *createTree* method. Then we print the result of creating the tree and print the results of preorder, inorder, and postorder traversals so that we can compare. This completes the binary tree traversal implementation.

```scala
package com.equalinformation.dascala.scala.bin_trees

object BinTreeTraversal {
  def main(args: Array[String]): Unit = {
    val myList = List(1,2,3,4,5,6)
    val myBinTree = createTree(myList)
    println(myBinTree)
    println(preorder(myBinTree))
    println(inorder(myBinTree))
    println(postorder(myBinTree))
  }

  def preorder[A](binTree: BinaryTree[A]): List[A] =
    binTree match {
      case Leaf => Nil
      case Branch(value, leftBranch, rightBranch) =>
        value :: (preorder(leftBranch) ++
        preorder(rightBranch))
    }

  def inorder[A](binTree: BinaryTree[A]): List[A] =
    binTree match {
      case Leaf => Nil
      case Branch(value, leftBranch, rightBranch) =>
        inorder(leftBranch) ++ (value :: inorder(rightBranch))
    }

  def postorder[A](binTree: BinaryTree[A]): List[A] =
    binTree match {
      case Leaf => Nil
      case Branch(value, leftBranch, rightBranch) =>
        postorder(leftBranch) ++ postorder(rightBranch) ++
        List(value)
    }

  def createTree[A](list: List[A]): BinaryTree[A] =
    list match {
      case Nil => Leaf
      case x :: xs => {
        val halfLength = xs.length / 2
        Branch(x, createTree(xs.take(halfLength)),
          createTree(xs.drop(halfLength)))
      }
    }
}
```

Fig. 8.2: Binary tree traversal

8.3 Analysis

We have seen a typical binary tree implementation, along with size and depth calculations. We also noticed that functional code is terse. The solutions to the exercises are in Appendix A. Next, we implemented three binary tree traversal algorithms—preorder, inorder, and postorder. We used recursive structures whenever there was an opportunity. Further, we observed the wide application of *List* in functional programming. The complete application is object-functional; however, most of our code is functional in nature.

8.4 Application

Binary trees have a wide variety of applications, which we will discuss later in this section. One of the specializations of binary trees is binary search trees, which make search applications faster. A binary tree is a binary search tree if the value at the root node is greater than or equal to all the values in the left subtree and less than or equal to all the values in the right subtree. This applies to all the nodes, which guarantees elements in an ascending order and this makes the search time complexity $O(lg\ n)$.

We present a dictionary application using a binary search tree in Figure 8.3. Let's discuss algorithms and their implementation together. First, we define a type *Dictionary*, which is a *BinaryTree* that takes a tuple, $(String, A)$, as a type. Note that the tuple itself has a generic type A. That means the key is going to be a *String* but the value can be any type. We also define *empty*, which is a *Leaf*. In the main method, we first create a list of key-value tuples; keys are some random words and values are some random numbers. We are creating an arbitrary dictionary of words in which we can experiment with insertion, search, update, etc. Next, we create a binary search tree by making use of the *insert* method. This is followed by applying three traversal methods to the tree so that we can verify whether the binary tree was constructed, and then we search for a specific word in the dictionary.

The *insert* method takes a key, a value, and a dictionary and returns a dictionary. If it finds an empty slot, *Leaf*, it inserts a branch with a node value $(key,\ value)$, and left and right subtrees as *Leaf*. The second case matches the input key with the current node's k value. If it matches then we have an existing key: no insertion is required and hence the error message. The third case is that in which the incoming key is less than the key value of the current node. Since it proceeds recursively, it finds the right place to insert, which is in the left subtree. During recursion two things happen—match or no match. If a match occurs it falls to the second case: key already present. If a match doesn't occur it falls to the first case, in which it creates a branch, as mentioned earlier. The last case does the same but on the right subtree, because the incoming key is greater than the existing key, k.

Now, let's analyze the *searchKey* method. If we hit the *Leaf*, that means the key is not found, so it returns *None*. If there is a match between the incoming key and the current key then it returns the value associated with that key with the help of a wrapper, *Some*, because our return type is *Option*[*A*]. If the incoming key is less than the current key, the method continues searching in the left subtree. If the incoming key is greater than the current key, the method continues searching in the right subtree. At some point it might match. If it does, it hits the second case. If it doesn't then it hits the first case.

Now, analyzing the *updateValue* method, it takes a key, a value to update to, and a dictionary in which the update is performed and then returns an updated dictionary. If the key is not found, it just inserts the incoming tuple (*key, value*); otherwise it replaces the value associated with the current key. This happens in the second case. The third case is the case in which the incoming key is less than the current key, and hence recursion continues on the left branch. If the incoming key is greater than the current key, the recursion continues in the right branch

Binary trees are used in compilers to process expressions using expression trees. Also they can be used for data compression, such as Huffman coding trees. One specialization of binary trees, binary search trees, discussed above, can be used to enhance search applications, since it supports search, insertion, and deletion with an average time complexity of $O(lg\ n)$.

```scala
package com.equalinformation.dascala.scala.bin_trees
object BinarySearchTreeApp {
  type Dictionary[A] = BinaryTree[(String, A)]
  def empty[A](): Dictionary[A] = Leaf
  def main(args: Array[String]): Unit = {
    val myWordList = List(("cat", 5), ("dog", 7),
      ("the", 12), ("for", 4), ("then", 11))
    val myBinSearchTree = myWordList.foldLeft(empty[Int]())
      ((y, x) => insert(x._1, x._2, y))
    println(inorder(myBinSearchTree))
    println(preorder(myBinSearchTree))
    println(postorder(myBinSearchTree))
    println(searchKey("for", myBinSearchTree))
  }
  def insert[A](key: String, value: A, dict: Dictionary[A]):
    Dictionary[A] = dict match {
    case Leaf => Branch((key, value), Leaf, Leaf)
    case Branch((k, v), lb, rb) if (key == k) =>
      sys.error(s"key ${key} already present")
    case Branch((k, v), lb, rb) if (key < k) =>
      Branch((k, v), insert(key, value, lb), rb)
    case Branch((k, v), lb, rb) if (key > k) =>
      Branch((k, v), lb, insert(key, value, rb))
  }
  def searchKey[A](key: String, dict: Dictionary[A]):
    Option[A] = dict match {
    case Leaf => None
    case Branch((k, v), lb, rb) if (key == k) => Some(v)
    case Branch((k, v), lb, rb) if (key < k) =>
      searchKey(key, lb)
    case Branch((k, v), lb, rb) if (key > k) =>
      searchKey(key, rb)
  }
  def updateValue[A](key: String, value: A,
    dict: Dictionary[A]): Dictionary[A] = dict match {
    case Leaf => Branch((key, value), Leaf, Leaf)
    case Branch((k, v), lb, rb) if (key == k) =>
      Branch((k, value), lb, rb)
    case Branch((k, v), lb, rb) if (key < k) =>
      Branch((k, value), updateValue(key, value, lb), rb)
    case Branch((k, v), lb, rb) if(key > k) =>
      Branch((k, value), lb, updateValue(key, value, rb))
  }
  def preorder[A](binTree: BinaryTree[A]): List[A] =
    binTree match {
    // preorder body here
  }

  def inorder[A](binTree: BinaryTree[A]): List[A] =
    binTree match {
    // inorder body here
  }

  def postorder[A](binTree: BinaryTree[A]): List[A] =
    binTree match {
    // postorder body here
  }
}
```

Fig. 8.3: Binary search tree application

Chapter 9
Sorting

Sorting is a common operation both in life and in computer science. In our daily life, we sort items so that searching is faster, and this is true in computer science as well. After all, computers exist to help us in our day-to-day tasks. There might be sorting present at different levels, based on requirements. For example, sometimes, we might need to sort character by character. At other times, we might need to sort larger structures, like company profiles. Whatever the reason, the basic principle of sorting remains same. Also, there are two orders for sorting—ascending and descending.

Let's assume that there are n items to be sorted: $< a_1, a_2, a_3, ..., a_n >$. When these items are sorted in ascending order their relationship can be formally stated as $a_1 \leq a_2 \leq a_3 \leq ... \leq a_n$. Similarly, their descending order sorting can be formally stated as $a_n \geq a_{n-1} \geq a_{n-2} \geq a_2 \geq a_1$.

9.1 Bubble Sort

9.1.1 Algorithm

Let's first outline the bubble sort algorithm:

1. Start with the first element in the sequence.
2. Compare the first element with the second element.
3. If the first element is greater than the second element then swap, else move on to the next element, which is the second element.
4. Compare the second element with the third element.
5. if the second element is greater than the third element then swap two, else move on to the third element, which is the next element in the input sequence.
6. Repeat the above steps until the second last element is compared with the last element, which completes the first pass and places the largest number in n^{th} po-

© Springer Nature Switzerland AG 2019
B. P. Upadhyaya, *Data Structures and Algorithms with Scala*, Undergraduate
Topics in Computer Science, https://doi.org/10.1007/978-3-030-12561-5_9

sition, i.e., the last position. If the indexing starts with 0 then it is position $n-1$. The first pass is completed with $(n-1)$ comparisons.

7. In the second pass, carry out similar operations until the third last element is compared with the second last element. We don't compare the last element because that is the largest element. So the second pass gives us the second largest element, which is stored in the second last position. The number of comparisons required for the second pass is $(n-2)$.

8. Repeat the above procedure until the final pass. In the final pass, we just need to compare two elements, i.e.: the first element and the second element. So the number of comparisons for the final pass is 1. After the final pass, we have a fully sorted sequence of elements, in ascending order.

9. During each comparison, instead of moving the larger one to the right, if we move the smaller one to the right we get the elements sorted in descending order.

9.1.2 Typical Implementation

We present a typical implementation of bubble sort in Figure 9.1. Let's first analyze the *calcMax* method. Remember that we calculated maximum in each pass in our algorithmic outline, in the previous section. If the input data matches *Nil*, then we don't have the maximum, and we just do the formality of *Nil* processing. If the input matches the second case, then the input has only one element. In that case, the maximum is the same element and the tail will be *Nil*. In the last case, we first calculate the maximum of tail and store the result in memory. Note that the result has two parts—tail maximum and remaining tail, i.e., tail of tail. If tail maximum is greater than or equal to head, tail maximum becomes the maximum and head becomes part of the remaining tail. Otherwise, head is the maximum and tail maximum stays with the remaining tail.

Now, let's analyze the *bubbleSortAsc* method. An empty list has nothing to sort so we return *Nil*. If the input list is not empty then we first calculate the maximum of all the elements and store the result in memory. The result has two parts, the maximum value and the remaining data. The remaining data, in the first iteration, is one less element from the input data list. Next, we apply *bubbleSortAsc* recursively on the remaining data and the maximum element from each iteration is concatenated. When recursion completes, we get a fully sorted list, in ascending order. This completes the bubble sort, in ascending order.

Exercise 9.1. *Bubble Sort: Descending Order*

Modify the application in Figure 9.1 to implement descending order.

```scala
package com.equalinformation.dascala.scala.sorting

object BubbleSortAscApp {
   def main(args: Array[String]): Unit = {
      println(bubbleSortAsc(List(3,1,6,8,2)))
      println(bubbleSortAsc(List("z", "c", "a", "b")))
   }

   def bubbleSortAsc[T <% Ordered[T]](myData: List[T]):
     List[T] = myData match {
     case Nil => Nil
     case _ => {
        val (max, remainingData) = calcMax(myData)
        bubbleSortAsc(remainingData) ::: List(max)
     }
   }

   def calcMax[T <% Ordered[T]](myData: List[T]): (T,
     List[T]) = myData match {
     case (Nil) => (null.asInstanceOf[T], Nil)
     case (head :: Nil) => (head, Nil)
     case (head :: tail) => {
        val (tailMax, tailRemaining) = calcMax(tail)
        if (tailMax >= head) (tailMax, head :: tailRemaining)
        else (head, tailMax :: tailRemaining)
     }
   }

}
```

Fig. 9.1: A typical bubble sort implementation

Exercise 9.2. *Bubble Sort: Generic*

Combine the solution of the above exercise, Exercise 9.1, with the implementation in
Figure 9.1 to create a generic bubble sort implementation. In your implementation,
you should have only one method called *bubbleSort* that does both ascending and
descending orders. From the main method, users of your application should be able
to pass a list and an order type as parameters.

9.2 Selection Sort

9.2.1 Algorithm

We outline the selection sort algorithm first:

1. Find the smallest element, or largest element if doing descending order, in the list and swap with the first element.
2. In the second pass, find the smallest element in the remaining list, which is a sublist of the given list that doesn't have the global smallest element.
3. Swap the smallest element with the lowest index in the sublist if the lowest index element is greater than this smallest element.
4. Continue the above steps until two elements are left in the list, which is the final pass, requiring only one comparison. Swap if the element at the lower index is greater than the element at the higher index. This completes selection sort.

9.2.2 Typical Implementation

We present a typical implementation of selection sort in Figure 9.2. Now, let's analyze the method *selectionSortAsc*. It takes a list of generic type of data as its input and returns a sorted list of the same type in ascending order. The first case returns *Nil* for an empty list. If the list contains only one element, then it is already sorted. This is covered by the second case, which returns a list of the head element.

Now, the interesting part: the third case covers an input case with two or more elements. First, the minimum of *tail* is calculated and also the corresponding index is recorded. If *head* is less than or equal to the minimum element of the tail then *head* is appended to the list returned by recursive *selectionSortAsc*. This guarantees that the smallest element is at the lowest index. If *head* is greater than the minimum element of the tail then *tail* is split at the index of the minimum element of the tail. This lets us pick the minimum, which is the head of the second half of the tail. Hence the head of the second half of the tail is appended to the recursive *selectSortAsc*. Now the new parameterized list is the concatenation of first half of the tail and the head prepended with the second half of the tail. Note that the head has been swapped with the minimum of the tail. This completes the selection sort, in ascending order.

In the *main* method, we call *selectionSortAsc* twice by passing two different types of lists—a list of integers and a list of strings. If the implementation is correct, it should be able to produce the sorted output for both types because we have used a generic type as an input to the sorting method, *selectionSortAsc*.

Exercise 9.3. *Selection Sort: Descending Order*

Modify the application in Figure 9.2 to implement selection sort in descending order.

```
package com.equalinformation.dascala.scala.sorting

object SelectionSortAscApp {
   def main(args: Array[String]): Unit = {
      println(selectionSortAsc(List(5,3,2,8,7)))
      println(selectionSortAsc(List("k","d","c","a","q")))
   }

   def selectionSortAsc[T <% Ordered[T]](myData: List[T]):
     List[T] = myData match {
      case Nil => Nil
      case head :: Nil => List(head)
      case head :: tail => {
         val minElem = tail.min
         val indexOfMinElem =
           tail.indexOf(minElem)
         if(head <= minElem) {
            head :: selectionSortAsc(tail)
         } else {
            val (tailHalf1, tailHalf2) =
              tail.splitAt(indexOfMinElem)
            tailHalf2.head :: selectionSortAsc(tailHalf1 :::
              head :: tailHalf2.tail)
         }
      }
   }
}
```

Fig. 9.2: A typical selection sort implementation

Exercise 9.4. *Selection Sort: Generic

Combine the solution of Exercise 9.3 with the implementation in Figure 9.2 to create
a generic selection sort implementation. A user of your implementation should be
able to perform both ascending and descending order selection sorts by calling a
single *selectionSort* method or function. They should be able to parameterize the
order type while calling your service.

9.3 Insertion Sort

9.3.1 Algorithm

We outline the insertion sort algorithm below.

1. The base case for insertion sort is the first element, which is sorted by default as it is the only element in a sublist of the input list. So, in the first pass, we compare the second element with the first element and if the second element is less than the first element we insert it before the first element. Now the first two elements are sorted and this is the sorted sublist for the second pass for the third element to be inserted in the correct place. The total number of comparisons required in the first pass, is one.
2. In the second pass, we take the third element and compare it with the elements in the sorted sublist from the first pass and insert it into the correct place. The total number of comparisons required in this pass is two.
3. We repeat the procedure for the rest of the remaining elements in the input list. In the last pass, the total number of comparisons required is $(n-1)$.

9.3.2 Typical Implementation

In Figure 9.3 we present a typical implementation of insertion sort. Let's first look at the *insertElementAsc* method. This method takes an element to be inserted and a sorted sublist where the element has to be inserted. If the sorted sublist is empty, we return the element prepended to it so that it forms a list of one element. If the sorted list has two or more elements, we split it into head and tail so that we can compare and insert the element under consideration. If the head is less than or equal to the element then the element must be inserted after the head, i.e., head comes first in the sorted sublist and hence is prepended to the recursive structure. If the element is less than the head then the element is prepended to the sorted sublist.

Now, let's look at the *insertionSortAsc* method. This method takes a list of elements as input and returns a sorted list for the same set of elements. If the incoming list is empty then we return that, as we don't have to sort. Otherwise, we split the incoming data into head and tail. We store the recursive call result in *temp*, which becomes a sorted list. Then we insert the head into this sorted list.

Now, in the *main* method, we first call *insertSortAsc* by passing a list of integers. This sorts the elements of type integer. Next, we vary the type of the elements by passing a list of strings. This time it sorts strings. This demonstrates the generic nature of our implementation in terms of data type.

Exercise 9.5. *Insertion Sort: Descending Order*

Modify the application in Figure 9.3 to implement descending order for insertion sort.

```
package com.equalinformation.dascala.scala.sorting

object InsertionSortAscApp {
   def main(args: Array[String]): Unit = {
     println(insertionSortAsc(List(15,10,33,11)))
     println(insertionSortAsc(List("banana","apple","mango")))
   }

   def insertionSortAsc[T <% Ordered[T]](myData: List[T]):
     List[T] = {
     if (myData == Nil) {
        myData
     } else {
        val head :: tail = myData
        val temp = insertionSortAsc(tail)
        insertElementAsc(head, temp)
     }
   }

   def insertElementAsc[T <% Ordered[T]](elem: T,
     sortedSubList: List[T]): List[T] = {
     if (sortedSubList == Nil) {
        return elem :: sortedSubList
     } else {
        val head :: tail = sortedSubList
        if (head <= elem) {
           head :: insertElementAsc(elem, tail)
        } else {
           elem :: sortedSubList
        }
     }
   }

}
```

Fig. 9.3: A typical insertion sort implementation

Exercise 9.6. *Insertion Sort: Generic*

Combine your solution Exercise 9.5 with the implementation in Figure 9.3 so as to create a generic insertion sort implementation. Your generic implementation should provide a single method or function, *insertionSort*, that can be called for both ascending as well as descending order sorting. You may parameterize the order type so that users of your application can specify the order as a parameter along with a list to be sorted.

9.4 Merge Sort

9.4.1 Algorithm

Let's outline the merge sort algorithm first. We can implement it in the next section. The algorithm below uses a divide and conquer strategy.

1. Split the given list till every sublist has at most one element.

   a. If the given data is an empty list then return two empty sublists.
   b. For a non-empty list, split the list into head and tail.
   c. If the tail is empty, then return two sublists, the first is the list with the head and the second is an empty list.
   d. If the given list has two or more elements then calculate the head of the tail and the tail of the tail of the given list. Next, split the tail of the tail of the given list into two parts—*part*1 and *part*2. Now, return two sublists so that the first sublist is formed by prepending the head of the given list to *part*1 and the second sublist is formed by prepending the head of the tail of the given list to *part*2.

2. Merge the sublists. While doing so, keep the merged list sorted too.

   a. The precondition is that the sublists should be sorted. If either the first sublist or the second sublist is empty then return the merged list, which is equal to the non-empty sublist.
   b. If both the sublists are non-empty then carry out the following.
      i. If the head of the first sublist is greater than the head of the second sublist then prepend the head of the second sublist to the recursive merge of the first list with the tail of the second sublist.
      ii. If the head of the second sublist is greater than or equal to the head of the first sublist then prepend the head of the first sublist to the recursive merge of the tail of the first sublist with the second sublist.

9.4.2 Typical Implementation

We present a typical implementation of merge sort in Figure 9.4. Let's first discuss the *split* method. It takes a list and returns two sublists. If the given list is empty then we return two sublists that are empty too. Next, we calculate the head and the tail of the given list so that it can be processed further for splitting. If the tail of the given list is empty then return the first sublist by prepending the head with *Nil*. In this case, the second sublist is *Nil*. Now, if the incoming list has two or more elements, we need to go through a slightly different process for splitting. First calculate the head of the tail and the tail of the tail of the given list. Then split the tail of the tail of the given list into two parts—*tailOfTailOfmyDataSplit*1 and *tailOfTailOfmyDataSplit2*. The first sublist to be returned is formed by prepending the head of the given list to the first split, above. Similarly, the second sublist to be returned is formed by prepending the head of the tail of the given list to the second split, above. This completes the splitting process.

Next, let's discuss the merging process, the method *mergeAsc*. This method takes two sorted lists—*sortedSubList1* and *sortedSubList2*—and returns a single merged list, which is sorted too. If one of the incoming lists is empty then the merged list is equal to the non-empty incoming list. If both *sortedSubList1* and *sortedSubList2* are non-empty then we compare their head elements. Whichever is the smaller, we prepend that to the recursive merge of the other sublist with the tail of the sublist whose head is smaller. This guarantees ascending order.

Now, let's look at the method *mergeSortAsc*. It takes a list and returns a sorted list, in ascending order. If the incoming list or its tail is empty then we return the list as it is because it can contain at most one element, which is sorted by default. Otherwise, we split the list and apply *mergeSortAsc* to each of the splits. The results are two sorted sublists. Next, we apply *mergeAsc*, which merges the two sorted sublists and keeps the order in the merged list, which is returned to the caller.

Finally, in our *main* method, we have two different calls to *mergeSortAsc*. The first call provides a list of integers and the second one provides a list of strings. Both are sorted because our implementation is generic, in terms of type. This completes the merge sort implementation for ascending order.

Exercise 9.7. *Merge Sort: Descending Order*

Modify the implementation in Figure 9.4 so as to implement descending order for merge sort.

Exercise 9.8. **Merge Sort: Generic*

Combine your solution for Exercise 9.7 with the implementation in Figure 9.4 to create a generic merge sort implementation. In your generic solution, there should be only one method called *mergeSort* that does both ascending and descending order sorting. You may parameterize the order type so that a user of your service can pass the order type along with data to be sorted.

```scala
package com.equalinformation.dascala.scala.sorting

object MergeSortAscApp {
  def main(args: Array[String]): Unit = {
    println(mergeSortAsc(List(5,6,2,3,1)))
    println(mergeSortAsc(List("cat", "put", "bag")))
  }

  def mergeSortAsc[T <% Ordered[T]](myData: List[T]):
    List[T] = {
    if( myData == Nil || myData.tail == Nil) {
      return myData
    }

    val (myDataSplit1, myDataSplit2) = split(myData)
    val sortedSL1 = mergeSortAsc(myDataSplit1)
    val sortedSL2 = mergeSortAsc(myDataSplit2)
    mergeAsc(sortedSL1, sortedSL2)
  }

  def mergeAsc[T <% Ordered[T]](sortedSubList1: List[T],
    sortedSubList2: List[T]): List[T] = (sortedSubList1,
    sortedSubList2) match {
    case (sortedSubList1, Nil) => sortedSubList1
    case (Nil, sortedSubList2) => sortedSubList2
    case (x1 :: y1, x2 :: y2) =>
      if (x1 > x2) x2 :: mergeAsc(sortedSubList1, y2)
      else x1 :: mergeAsc(y1, sortedSubList2)
  }

  def split[T <% Ordered[T]](myData: List[T]): (List[T],
    List[T]) = {
    if (myData == Nil) {
      return (Nil, Nil)
    }

    val headOfmyData = myData.head
    val tailOfmyData = myData.tail
    if(tailOfmyData == Nil) {
      return (headOfmyData :: Nil, Nil)
    }
    val headOfTailOfmyData = tailOfmyData.head
    val tailOfTailOfmyData = tailOfmyData.tail
    val (tailOfTailOfmyDataSplit1, tailOfTailOfmyDataSplit2)
      = split(tailOfTailOfmyData)
    return (headOfmyData :: tailOfTailOfmyDataSplit1,
      headOfTailOfmyData :: tailOfTailOfmyDataSplit2)
  }

}
```

Fig. 9.4: A typical merge sort implementation

9.5 Quick Sort

9.5.1 Algorithm

Let's first outline the algorithm for quick sort. Like merge sort, quick sort also benefits from the power of a divide and conquer strategy.

1. First, we select a pivot element in the given list. There are many ways to select a pivot, including randomization. Selection of the pivot determines the performance of quick sort. For simplicity, we take the first element as our pivot for the first pass. The second element will be the pivot for the second pass, and so on.
2. In the first pass, we create two sublists, i.e., all the elements smaller than the pivot will be on the first sublist and all the elements greater than the pivot will be on the second sublist. This gives us ascending order. If we reverse the logic, we get descending order.
3. In the second pass, we change our pivot, and the second element becomes the new pivot. Now, all the elements smaller than the second element will be part of the first partition and those that are greater will be part of the second partition. This process slowly sorts the elements. By the end of the second pass there will be at least two elements sorted. Note that it takes longer if the list is already sorted, which is the worst performance case for quick sort.
4. In every pass, elements either go to the left of the pivot or to the right. In order to create the final sorted list, we need to merge the left partition, the pivot, and the right partition. The pivot can be either appended to the left partition or prepended to the right partition in order to create a final sorted list. In Scala, prepending has constant time complexity whereas appending has $O(n)$ complexity. Certainly we would like to pick $O(1)$ complexity.

9.5.2 Typical Implementation

We present a typical implementation of the quick sort algorithm in Figure 9.5. Let's first discuss the method *partitionAsc*. It takes a pivot, a list to be partitioned, a left partition placeholder, and a right partition placeholder , as inputs. If the incoming list is empty then we return $p1$ and $p2$ unchanged; both are initialized as *Nil* from a calling LOC. If the head of the incoming list is less than the pivot then the head is prepended to the left partition, $p1$, otherwise it is prepended to the right partition. This is applied recursively. This gives us an ascending order.

Now, let's look at the *quickSortAsc* method. It takes a list to be sorted as an input and produces a sorted list as its output. If the incoming list is empty then we return *Nil*. If the incoming list has only one element then we return a list containing that element. If the incoming list has two or more elements then we partition the list. When we partition, we get two parts—a left partition and a right partition. Then we prepend the head to the right partition because prepend has complexity of $O(1)$

whereas append has complexity of $O(n)$. Finally, we combine the left partition with the right partition, which has the head prepended to it. This gives us a completely sorted list, in ascending order.

```
package com.equalinformation.dascala.scala.sorting

object QuickSortAsc {
    def main(args: Array[String]): Unit = {
        println(quickSortAsc(List(5,2,1,6,7)))
        println(quickSortAsc(List("grape","apple","apricot")))
    }

    def quickSortAsc[T <% Ordered[T]](myData: List[T]):
      List[T] = myData match {
        case Nil => Nil
        case head :: Nil => List(head)
        case head :: tail => {
            val (p1, p2) = partitionAsc(head, tail, Nil, Nil)
            val leftToPivot = quickSortAsc(p1)
            val rightToPivot = quickSortAsc(p2)
            val temp = head :: rightToPivot
            return leftToPivot ++ temp
        }
    }

    def partitionAsc[T <% Ordered[T]](pivot: T, myData:
      List[T], p1: List[T], p2: List[T]): (List[T], List[T]) =
      myData match {
        case Nil => (p1, p2)
        case head :: tail =>
            if (head < pivot) partitionAsc(pivot, tail, head ::
              p1, p2)
            else partitionAsc(pivot, tail, p1, head :: p2)
    }

}
```

Fig. 9.5: A typical quick sort implementation

Exercise 9.9. *Quick Sort: Descending Order*

Modify the implementation in Figure 9.5 to implement descending order for the quick sort algorithm presented in Section 9.5.1.

Exercise 9.10. *Quick Sort: Generic*

Combine the solution of Exercise 9.9 with the implementation in Figure 9.5 to create a generic implementation for the algorithm presented in Section 9.5.1. A user of your implementation should be able to perform both ascending and descending order quick sort by calling a single *quickSort* method or function. They should be able to parameterize the order type while calling your generic implementation of the quick sort algorithm.

9.6 Comparative Analysis

As described in Section 9.1.1, bubble sorts does $(n-1)$ comparisons in the first pass, where n is the number of elements in the input data sequence. In the second pass, it does $(n-2)$ comparisons to find the largest among the remaining elements; the largest among the whole sequence is already settled as the last element. In the final pass, we determine the smallest and the second smallest elements, which needs only one comparison. So the total number of comparisons required is $(n-1)+(n-2)+ \dots +1$, which evaluates to $\frac{n(n-1)}{2}$. So the time complexity of bubble sort is $O(n^2)$.

The first pass of selection sort makes $(n-1)$ comparisons, as described in the algorithm in Section 9.2.1. To find a smallest or largest element, it has to compare one element with rest of the elements. However, in the second pass, there is one less element to compare because the smallest in the input has already been identified and placed in the smallest index. So the second pass has to make only $(n-2)$ comparisons. Similarly, the final pass makes only one comparison. So the total number of comparisons required for selection sort is $(n-1)+(n-2)+ \dots +1$, which evaluates to $\frac{n(n-1)}{2}$. Hence, the time complexity of selection sort is $O(n^2)$.

In the case of insertion sort, we start with a sorted sublist and an element to be inserted. The initial sorted sublist consists of one element, the first element. Hence the number of comparisons required in the first pass is one. Similarly, the number of comparisons required in the second pass is two, because the first pass added one element in the sublist containing the first element. In the final pass, the number of comparisons required is $(n-1)$. Hence the total number of comparisons required for selection sort is $1+2+ \dots +(n-1)$, which is $\frac{n(n-1)}{2}$. Therefore, the time complexity of insertion sort is $O(n^2)$. In the best case, the input list might be already sorted. But we need to check whether the input list is actually sorted, and hence it has time complexity $O(n)$.

The merge sort algorithm is presented in Section 9.4.1. Since we are splitting the given list into sublists containing at most one element, it takes $O(n)$ time. Similarly, since merge is the opposite of splitting and we have n splits to merge, it has $O(n)$ time complexity. So, the splitting and merging combined time complexity is $O(n+n) = O(2n)$ and this is equivalent to $O(n)$. There is one more time complexity, i.e., both merging and splitting deal with a height of $lg\ n$. This gives us the total time complexity of merge sort as $O(n\ lg\ n)$.

Lastly, the quick sort algorithm presented in Section 9.5.1 gives a good indication of the time complexity. On average, quick sort has to deal with $(lg\ n)$ height and each step has $O(n)$ complexity. This gives us an average time complexity for quick sort of $O(n\ lg\ n)$. Ironically, for quick sort, the worst case is when the input list is already sorted. In that case, the algorithm has to deal with n height. So the total worst case time complexity for quick sort is $O(n^2)$. This completes our analysis of all five sorting algorithms. Finally, Table 9.1 presents a summary of our discussion.

Table 9.1: Time complexities of sorting algorithms

Algorithm	Best Case	Average Case	Worst Case
Bubble sort	$O(n)$	$O(n^2)$	$O(n^2)$
Selection sort	$O(n^2)$	$O(n^2)$	$O(n^2)$
Insertion sort	$O(n)$	$O(n^2)$	$O(n^2)$
Merge sort	$O(n\ lg\ n)$	$O(n\ lg\ n)$	$O(n\ lg\ n)$
Quick sort	$O(n\ lg\ n)$	$O(n\ lg\ n)$	$O(n^2)$

9.7 Application

Sorting can help reduce the complexity of a problem. Let's think about searching an element in an unsorted array. We have to compare our search item with every element in the array under consideration. If the array has billions of elements in it, the search process is certainly going to be time-consuming. Not only that, as more elements are added to the array, the searching gets worse. One can think of a column of a database as an array, because database columns or rows are often represented as arrays for in-memory processing. There are higher-level data structures available, but arrays are faster. Even with this fastest data structure, searching is not efficient. It is a scalability problem.

Now, let's think about the same search problem in a sorted array. We could start from the middle of the array and then, depending upon whether the search element is less than or greater than the middle element, we can either go to the left of the array or to the right. In the first pass, we have reduced the search space by half. In the second pass, our search space will be one-quarter. So the search time complexity for a sorted array is $O(lg\ n)$, whereas it is $O(n)$ for unsorted array.

For companies like Google, Amazon, Apple, and Facebook the search has to go through petabytes of data. Sorting is certainly applied to improve performance. Sorting is also heavily used in databases internally.

Chapter 10
Searching

Searching is frequently used in our daily life as well as in computer science. If we are doing a manual search, most likely we try to match the image or description that we have in our brain to the actual object that we are looking for. So it is a kind of pattern matching operation. Similarly, pattern matching is a common technique used in computing too.

Now, let's discuss a couple of cases to set the stage for our searching algorithms. In the case of images, we do structural matching or comparison, i.e., each component in the target object is matched with the reference object that we have in our brain. The order is not unique as we apply visual inspection. Different people match in different ways. Largely, this depends upon our earlier training. This might also be enhanced with specific knowledge and rules. For example, there are rules for manufacturing coins. If one side of a coin matches the description, there is no need to match the other side, because it is governed by currency-specific rules.

The second case that we are interested is textual matching, which will be the focus of this chapter. In textual matching, substring searching is a very common requirement, and hence we will be dealing with those algorithms in the following sections. If we are doing a substring search manually, then we match the first character of the substring to be searched with the first character of the text in which we are performing matching. If that matches, we continue with the second character and so on. Since we can move our eyes, we could start by matching from the middle of a page or anywhere we like. But if we are looking for first occurrence then it will be a sequential match or search. In the case of computers, matching is generally performed sequentially. But this can be changed if we have different requirements.

Searching has a wide range of algorithms. Binary search trees are presented in Chapter 8. In this chapter, we will be dealing with *Naive* search and *Knuth-Morris-Pratt* search algorithms.

© Springer Nature Switzerland AG 2019
B. P. Upadhyaya, *Data Structures and Algorithms with Scala*, Undergraduate
Topics in Computer Science, https://doi.org/10.1007/978-3-030-12561-5_10

10.1 Algorithms

Let's first outline the *Naive* search algorithm.

1. For the first character in the text perform the following matching loop.

   a. Match the first character of the substring being searched with the current character of the text.
   b. If there is a match then match the second character of the substring with the next character of the text. Continue this until all the characters of the substring match with the characters of the text. If there is a complete match then return the index of the current character of the text, which is 0 in this case.
   c. If there is no match, then exit this matching loop.

2. Now, move the pointer to the second character of the text and carry on performing the matching loop described above. Any partial match is lost in the backtracking process. If there is a complete match, return the index, which is 1 in this case. If there is no complete match, move the pointer to the third character.

3. Continue the above steps until we reach an index which when added to the length of the substring gives the length of the text, i.e., the last starting point for comparison should have enough characters following it so that the index stays within the limit. In the worst case, the running time complexity of *Naive* search is $O(mn)$, where m is the length of the substring to be searched and n is the length of the text in which search is performed.

Now, let's outline the *Knuth-Morris-Pratt* algorithm.

1. Initialize variables.

   m = Length of the pattern (substring to be searched)
   n = Length of the text
   T = Prefix table
   i = Number of characters matched

2. Compute the prefix table first. This is a preprocess that processes the pattern to find matches of prefixes of the pattern with the pattern itself. The pattern here is a substring to be searched. It indicates how much of the last comparison can be reused if the comparison fails; this is an improvement over the *Naive* search algorithm. P and S denote the pattern to be searched and the text in which the search is performed, respectively. The prefix function is defined as the size of the largest prefix of $P[0, 1, ..., l-1]$ that is also a suffix of $P[1, 2, ..., l]$. The prefix table is computed with the help of the following subroutine, which has $O(m)$ running time complexity.

   a. $m \leftarrow length[P]$
   b. $T[1] \leftarrow 0$
   c. $k \leftarrow 0$
   d. **for** $l \leftarrow 2$ to m **do**
         while $k > 0$ and $P[k+1] \neq p[l]$ **do**
            $k \leftarrow T[k]$

end while
if $P[k+1] = P[l]$ **then**
    $k \leftarrow k+1$
end if
$T[l] \leftarrow k$
end for

e. **return** T

3. Perform variable initialization: $i = 0$ indicates the beginning of the match.
4. Compare the first character of the substring to be searched (pattern) with the first character of the text. If it is not a match substitute the value of $T[i]$ to i. If it is a match then increment the value of i by 1.
5. Next, check if all the pattern elements are matched with the text elements. If not matched then repeat the search process. If matched then return the starting index of the matched substring of the text.
6. Continue the above steps to find the next match.
7. The above steps can be represented by the following pseudo-code.

a. $n \leftarrow length[S]$
b. $m \leftarrow length[P]$
c. $T \leftarrow computePrefixTable(P)$, call prefix computation subroutine above.
d. $i \leftarrow 0$
e. **for** $j \leftarrow 1$ to n **do**
      while $i > 0$ and $P[i+1] \neq S[j]$ **do**
          $i \leftarrow T[i]$
          if $P[i+1] = S[j]$ **then**
              $i \leftarrow i+1$
          end if
          if $i = m$ **then**
              $i \leftarrow P[i]$
          end if
      end while
end for

8. Return a set of starting indices for all matched substrings of the text. The running time complexity of prefix table computation is $O(m)$. It takes $O(n)$ to compare the pattern to the text. Hence, the total running time complexity is $O(m+n)$.

In order to clarify the above algorithm, let's compute a prefix table for $P = \{xyxyxzx\}$. Initially, $m = length[P] = 7$, $T[1] = 0$, and $k = 0$. As shown in the algorithm above, m is the length of the pattern or string to be searched, T is the prefix table, and k is the initial potential value that is initialized to 0.

- Step 1: $l = 2$, $k = 0$, $T[2] = 0$

l	1	2	3	4	5	6	7
P	x	y	x	y	x	z	x
T	0	0					

- Step 2: $l = 3$, $k = 0$, $T[3] = 1$

l	1	2	3	4	5	6	7
P	x	y	x	y	x	z	x
T	0	0	1				

- Step 3: $l = 4$, $k = 1$, $T[4] = 2$

l	1	2	3	4	5	6	7
P	x	y	x	y	x	z	x
T	0	0	1	2			

- Step 4: $l = 5$, $k = 2$, $T[5] = 3$

l	1	2	3	4	5	6	7
P	x	y	x	y	x	z	x
T	0	0	1	2	3		

- Step 5: $l = 6$, $k = 3$, $T[6] = 1$

l	1	2	3	4	5	6	7
P	x	y	x	y	x	z	x
T	0	0	1	2	3	1	

- Step 6: $l = 7$, $k = 1$, $T[7] = 1$

l	1	2	3	4	5	6	7
P	x	y	x	y	x	z	x
T	0	0	1	2	3	1	1

Now, let's look at an example to realize the KMP algorithm. We have $P = \{xyxyxzx\}$ from the above analysis. Let's assume $S = \{yxzyxyxyxyxzxxy\}$. Now, let's walk through our KMP algorithm to check whether P occurs in S.

- Step 1: $j = 1$, $i = 0$, comparing $P[1]$ with $S[1]$. Since $P[1]$ does not match with $S[1]$, P is shifted one position to the right.

Text	y	x	z	y	x	y	x	y	x	y	x	z	x	x	y

Pattern	x	y	x	y	x	z	x

- Step 2: $j = 2$, $i = 0$, comparing $P[1]$ with $S[2]$, there is a match.

Text	y	x	z	y	x	y	x	y	x	y	x	z	x	x	y

Pattern	x	y	x	y	x	z	x

- Step 3: $j = 3$, $i = 1$, comparing $P[2]$ with $S[3]$, there is no match. Now, backtracking on P and comparing $P[1]$ with $S[3]$, that is not a match. So now proceed with the next character in S, by increasing the index to S.

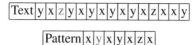

- Step 4: $j = 4$, $i = 0$, comparing $P[1]$ with $S[4]$, there is no match. Next, move on to the next index of S.

- Step 5: $j = 5$, $i = 0$, comparing $P[1]$ with $S[5]$, there is match. Since there is a match, increase the index of P as well for the next step.

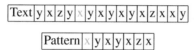

- Step 6: $j = 6$, $i = 1$, comparing $P[2]$ with $S[6]$, there is a match. For the next step, increase the index of P as well.

- Step 7: $j = 7$, $i = 2$, comparing $P[3]$ with $S[7]$, there is a match. So increase the index of P as well for the next step.

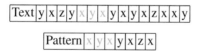

- Step 8: $j = 8$, $i = 3$, comparing $P[4]$ with $S[8]$, there is a match. For the next step, increase the index of P as well.

- Step 9: $j = 9$, $i = 4$, comparing $P[5]$ with $S[9]$, there is a match. So increase the index of P as well for the next step.

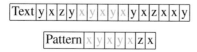

- Step 10: $j = 10$, $i = 5$, comparing $P[6]$ with $S[10]$, there is no match. So backtrack on P and compare $P[4]$ with $S[10]$ since mismatch resulted in $i = prefixValue[5] = 3$. Refer to the prefix calculation steps above. Since there is a match, increase the index of P as well for the next step.

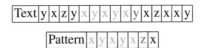

- Step 11: $j = 11$, $i = 4$, comparing $P[5]$ with $S[11]$, there is a match. Since there is a match, increase the index of P as well for the next step.

- Step 12: $j = 12$, $i = 5$, comparing $P[6]$ with $S[12]$, there is a match. Increase the index of P as well for the next step.

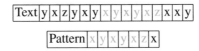

- Step 13: $j = 13$, $i = 6$, comparing $P[7]$ with $S[13]$. There is a match. Since we don't have any more characters left in P, this completes the process and we can return the index value, $value = currentIndex(S) + 1 - length(P) = 14 - 7 = 7$. For this example, the total number of shifts $= i - m = 13 - 7 = 6$.

10.2 Typical Implementation

We present a typical implementation of *Naive* search in Figure 10.1. Let's first analyze the method *naiveSubstringSearch*. It takes a string to be searched (pattern) and a string in which search is performed (text) as its parameters. It returns an index of the first occurrence of the pattern in the text. For the entire length of the data, we apply the *find* operation. In order to avoid an index out of bound condition we place a check, i.e., continue the matching operation if the current text index is less than or equal to the length of the text less the length of the pattern. This ensures there are sufficient characters for comparison. If this condition is met then we match each character of the pattern with the characters of the text. If there is a complete match then we return the index, otherwise we return -1.

In the *main* method, we create a sample text and a sample pattern. Next, we invoke *naiveSubstringSearch* and print the result. Since both the pattern and text are small, it convenient to verify this manually.

Exercise 10.1. *Imperative* **Naive** *Search Implementation*

Modify the solution presented in Figure 10.1 to provide an imperative solution.

```
package com.equalinformation.dascala.scala.searching

object NaiveSubstringSearchApp {
   def main(args: Array[String]): Unit = {
      val myData1 = "This is a functional implementation."
      val myWords1 = "functional"
      println(naiveSubstringSearch(myWords1, myData1))
   }

   def naiveSubstringSearch(myWords: String, myData:String):
     Int = {
     myData.indices.find { i =>
     i + myWords.length <= myData.length &&
     myWords.indices.forall(j => myData(j + i) == myWords(j))
     }.getOrElse(-1)
   }
}
```

Fig. 10.1: A typical *Naive* search implementation

Exercise 10.2. *Naive *Search All Occurrences*

Modify the implementation in Figure 10.1 so as to find all the occurrences of a given
pattern in a given text. Your implementation should print all the corresponding indices and the total count of all occurrences.

Next, let's discuss the KMP implementation. In Figure 10.2, we present a typical
KMP algorithm implementation. The method *prefixTable* computes the prefix table
for a given pattern. It has a *String* input and outputs a vector of integers, which is a
prefix table. We use *foldLeft*. The first item in the prefix table is always zero, hence
we start with a vector containing zero. Also, we skip the first character as it always
has an entry of zero, which we have already calculated. In this case, we extract our
initial state, which is a tuple containing an initial value and the prefix table. We
process the current character with this initial state. We iterate the stream starting
with our initial value and keep lowering the initial value as long as the condition is
satisfied. The function passed to the *find* operation checks whether the initial value
is zero or the current character matches search string's currently indexed character.
Next, we increase the lower value if the result of *searchString(lowerValue)* matches
with *currentCharacter*, otherwise the new value is same as the lower value. Next,
we return the tuple containing new value and the vector that has the new value added
into it. Finally, we return the vector, which is the second element in the tuple. This
completes the prefix table computation.

Next, let's discuss the operation *kmpSubstringSearch*, which is an implementation of the KMP algorithm. First, we create the prefix table by calling the operation *prefixTable*. Next, we write the main logic. Again we use *foldLeft* with
initial condition $(-1,0)$. The first element of this tuple, -1, represents the index

when the pattern is found, and the second element represents the initial value of the length of the match. We run the logic for all the characters in the text and hence *myData.indices*. We have two cases to cover. For both cases, *foundIndex* represents an index when a match occurs, *x* represents the current matches, and *i* represents the current index from the range of indices of the text. The first case covers the "found" case. If the pattern is found then we return a tuple containing *foundIndex* and 0. The second element of the tuple doesn't matter, so we simply return 0. In the second case, we do stream iteration, which is similar to a *while* loop. We iterate with initial value *x*, and each time *s* is assigned a new value using *prefixTab*$(x-1)$. The value of *lowerX* provides a stopping condition. Our conditions are either $x == 0$ or there is a match. Since *find* returns an *Option*, we need to use *get* to get the corresponding value. Next, *newX* is increased by one if there is a match, otherwise it is left as it is. The last LOC checks if it is a complete match. If it is, then it returns a tuple containing *foundIndex* and 0. If it is not a complete match, then it returns -1 for *foundIndex*, indicating that we have not found the pattern. The second element of the tuple is *newX*. Finally, since the *foldLeft* returns a tuple, we are interested in the first element, because the first element gives the *foundIndex*.

In the *main* method, we define two strings—text and pattern. Then we print the result of invoking the *kmpSubstringSearch* method. If the pattern is found, then the relevant index is printed, otherwise -1 is the output. This completes the KMP implementation.

```scala
package com.equalinformation.dascala.scala.searching

object KnuthMorrisPrattApp {
  def main(args: Array[String]): Unit = {
    val myData1 = "This is a functional implementation."
    val myWords1 = "functional"
    println(kmpSubstringSearch(myWords1, myData1))
  }

  def kmpSubstringSearch(myWords: String, myData:String):
    Int = {
    val prefixTab = prefixTable(myWords)

    myData.indices.foldLeft(-1, 0) {
        case ((foundIndex, x), i) if foundIndex > 0 =>
          (foundIndex, 0)
        case ((foundIndex, x), i) => {
          val stepsX = Stream.iterate(x)(x => prefixTab(x-1))
          val lowerX = stepsX.find(x => x == 0 || myWords(x)
            == myData(i)).get
          val newX = if (myWords(lowerX) == myData(i))
            lowerX + 1 else lowerX
          if(newX == myWords.length) (i - newX + 1, 0) else
            (-1, newX)
        }
    }._1
  }

  def prefixTable(searchString: String): Vector[Int] = {
    searchString.drop(1).foldLeft(0, Vector(0)) {
        case ((initialValue, prefixT), currentCharacter) => {
          val lowerValue = Stream.iterate(initialValue)(
            initialValue => prefixT(initialValue - 1))
            .find(initialValue => initialValue == 0 ||
            searchString(initialValue) == currentCharacter)
            .get
          val newValue = if (searchString(lowerValue) ==
            currentCharacter) lowerValue + 1 else lowerValue

          (newValue, prefixT :+ newValue)
        }
    }._2
  }

}
```

Fig. 10.2: A typical implementation for *Knuth-Morris-Pratt* algorithm

10.3 Analysis

We picked two algorithms for our discussions in this chapter. The *Naive* search has a running time of $O(mn)$, where m is the length of the pattern and n is the length of the text. This algorithm does backtracking when a complete match doesn't occur. This becomes inefficient when there are numerous partial matches. The KMP algorithm avoids backtracking by computing a prefix table. It can re-use the last partial match for the next iteration, thereby avoiding re-computation. The running time complexity of KMP algorithm is $O(n)$.

10.4 Application

Searching is ubiquitous. We search words in dictionaries. We might search names and phone numbers in a phone directory. We search different things using Internet search engines such as Google. All of these searches perform some kind of matching. It can be: pattern matching, key matching, etc. In all cases the logic from KMP or *Naive* search can be utilized. Since KMP has $O(n)$ running time compared to *Naive*'s $O(mn)$ it can be utilized to implement faster substring searching, specially when we are building search applications from scratch.

Chapter 11
Graphs

Graph structures are common. For example, if we represent each city with a circle and the roads connecting to them with a line, we get a graph. Generally, the traffic is bidirectional, so we get an undirected or bidirectional graph. Similarly, if we create a diagram based on flights between cities, we get another graph. Further, the interaction among people can be represented by graphs. So graphs are commonly available structures.

11.1 Structure and Algorithms

In terms of structure, a graph is a nonlinear structure that has two parts:

1. A set $V = V(G)$ whose elements are called vertices, nodes, or points of G.
2. A set $E = E(G)$ of unordered pairs of distinct vertices called edges or arcs of G.

Hence, a graph can be represented as a tuple $G = (V, E)$, where V is a set of vertices, nodes, or points and E is a set of edges or arcs..

Similarly, a directed graph or digraph is a nonlinear structure in which the edges are one-way, which has two parts:

1. A set $V = V(G)$ whose elements are called vertices, nodes, or points of G.
2. A set $E = E(G)$ of ordered pairs (a, b) of vertices called directed edges or arcs. Directed edges are sometimes called simply edges.

In this chapter, we will be dealing with directed graphs, simply called graphs. So, Let's discuss the conventions that we will be using. Suppose $e = (a, b)$ is a directed edge in a digraph G. We will use the following conventions:

1. e begins at a and ends at b.
2. a is the origin or initial point of e, and b is the destination or end point of e.
3. b is a successor of a.
4. a is adjacent to b, and b is adjacent to a.

© Springer Nature Switzerland AG 2019
B. P. Upadhyaya, *Data Structures and Algorithms with Scala*, Undergraduate
Topics in Computer Science, https://doi.org/10.1007/978-3-030-12561-5_11

There are two common algorithms to traverse a graph—depth-first and breadth-first. In depth-first, a node's children are visited before its siblings. In the case of breadth-first, a node's siblings are visited before its children.

11.2 Typical Implementation

We present a typical implementation of a graph in Figure 11.1. A graph can be represented with the help of lists.

```
val myGraph = List(("a", "b"), ("a", "c"), ("b", "d"),
("b", "e"), ("b", "c"), ("c", "e"), ("d", "f"))
```

In the above code snippet, letters represent graph vertices or nodes and tuples represent graph edges. For example, ("a", "b") represents an edge from vertex a to vertex b. Similarly, ("a", "c") represents an edge from vertex a to vertex c. So vertex a connects to vertex b and c. The rest of the tuples can be interpreted in the same way.

Now, let's look at the method *calcSuccessorSet*, which calculates a successor set of a vertex. An adjacent vertex in the direction of the arrow is a successor. A successor set is a non-repeating collection of such adjacent vertices. For example, the successor set of vertex a is $\{b, c\}$. In the *calSuccessorSet*, the case *Nil* covers the empty list or that there are no more vertices to calculate successor for. The second case checks if *vertex* matches the first element of the tuple; if it matches, then the second element is added to the successor set. The last case is the default case of no match and it skips the current tuple. We will be using *calcSuccessorSet* in other programs in this chapter. For example, to traverse a graph, we need to calculate successors; similarly, to perform topological sorting, we need to do the same.

In Figure 11.2, we present depth-first and breadth-first traversals. Let's look at the method *traverseDepthFirst*. It takes the starting point or starting vertex and then the graph, which is a list of tuples. Each tuple represents an arc in the graph; the relevant vertices are included implicitly. The method returns a list of vertices, which is a list of *String*, in this implementation. Note that we have the private method *depthFirst*, because we don't want to expose the details outside. Also, this particular implementation avoids list appending, which is expensive.

The inner method *depthFirst* takes a list of vertices and a list of visited vertices, and returns a list of vertices as a result of depth-first traversal. The first case covers the case that there are no more edges to traverse and the list of visited vertices is returned. The second case does the magic of traversal. It applies *depthFirst* recursively by passing suitable parameters. The first parameter is the remaining vertices in the list of vertices. If a vertex has already been visited then the second parameter is the visited list. If the vertex was not visited then a depth-first traversal must be performed on its successors and the current vertex becomes part of the visited list. This completes depth-first traversal.

```
package com.equalinformation.dascala.scala.graphs

object GraphApp {
    def main(args: Array[String]): Unit = {
        val myGraph = List(("a", "b"), ("a", "c"), ("b", "d"),
            ("b", "e"), ("b", "c"), ("c", "e"), ("d", "f"))

        println(calcSuccessorSet("b", myGraph))
    }

    def calcSuccessorSet(vertex: String, graph:
      List[(String, String)]): List[String] = graph match {
        case Nil => Nil
        case x :: xs if (vertex == x._1) => x._2 ::
          calcSuccessorSet(vertex, xs)
        case _ :: xs => calcSuccessorSet(vertex, xs)
    }
}
```

Fig. 11.1: A typical graph implementation

Now, let's look at the method *traverseBreadthFirst*. The parameter lists are similar to that of *traverseDepthFirst* method. Also we have a parallel private method called *breadthFirst*. When there are no more edges to traverse the list of visited vertices is returned, which is covered by the first case. The second case or clause matches when *x* is already a member of the visited list of vertices. In this case, the current vertex is skipped because it has already been visited. The last case matches when *x* is encountered for the first time. Here, the list of vertices to be processed is formed by appending successors of the current vertex to the remaining vertices in the list. Since successors are appended, the children's breadth-first traversal is done later relative to the siblings' breadth-first traversal. This guarantees breadth-first traversal.

Exercise 11.1. *Performance Improvement of Breadth-First*

In Figure 11.2, *traverseBreadhFirst* uses list appending, which is an expensive operation in general. Improve this method by eliminating list appending. Hint: see the implementation of the method *traverseDepthFirst*; a similar technique might work.

```scala
package com.equalinformation.dascala.scala.graphs

object GraphTraversalApp {
  def main(args: Array[String]): Unit = {
    val myGraph = List(("a", "b"), ("a", "c"), ("b", "d"),
      ("b", "e"), ("b", "c"), ("c", "e"), ("d", "f"))
    println(traverseDepthFirst("a", myGraph))
    println(traverseBreadthFirst("a", myGraph))
  }

  def traverseDepthFirst(start: String, graph:
    List[(String, String)]): List[String] = {
    def depthFirst(vertices: List[String], visited:
      List[String]): List[String] = vertices match {
      case Nil => visited
      case x :: xs => depthFirst(xs,
          if(visited.contains(x)) visited
          else depthFirst(calcSuccessorSet(x, graph),
            x :: visited))
    }

    val result = depthFirst(List(start), List())
    result.reverse
  }

  def traverseBreadthFirst(start: String,
    graph: List[(String, String)]): List[String] = {
    def breadthFirst(vertices: List[String], visited:
      List[String]): List[String] = vertices match {
      case Nil => visited
      case x :: xs if visited.contains(x) =>
        breadthFirst(xs, visited)
      case x :: xs => breadthFirst(xs ++
        calcSuccessorSet(x, graph), x :: visited)
    }

    val result = breadthFirst(List(start), List())
    result.reverse
  }

  def calcSuccessorSet(vertex: String, graph:
    List[(String, String)]): List[String] = graph match {
    case Nil => Nil
    case x :: xs if (vertex == x._1) => x._2 ::
      calcSuccessorSet(vertex, xs)
    case _ :: xs => calcSuccessorSet(vertex, xs)
  }

}
```

Fig. 11.2: Graph traversal

11.3 Analysis

A typical graph implementation code using a list is succinct. In fact, almost all the code written primarily in functional style is terse, even though it might look a bit abstract in the beginning. We used list element prepend (::) in almost all the implementations in this chapter, primarily because it has better performance, i.e., the time complexity is $O(1)$. The two primary language constructs used were pattern matching and lists. We also made use of inner methods or private methods to hide the details. Note how inner methods are used; first they are defined and then invoked using a base case.

11.4 Application

Graphs have wide range of applications. Let's first look at one of those applications from an implementation point of view. Topological sorting is a specific type of sorting where items are sorted based on precedence. For example, we go to an elementary school first and then to a middle school, and finally we wrap up our K-12 education with a high school. If we are using a K-12 education system, an elementary school has to come before a middle school and a middle school has to come before a high school.

In Figure 11.3, we implement a topological sorting for events related to universities admission and graduation. *myEventList* contains a list of events as tuples. Each tuple represents two adjacent vertices in a corresponding graph. Since it is a directed graph, the arrow is from the first element of a tuple to the second element of that tuple. This much information is sufficient to construct a graph. The tuples information is related to precedence; however, there are alternate paths, and events in alternate paths should follow precedence when sorted. For example, whether we go to CMU or MIT, graduation comes after choosing a major. Similarly, in order to join either of these universities, we first need to receive an admission offer. To receive an admission offer, we first need to apply. Application is not complete if there is no test score, which means that we need to take standardized tests before completing our applications. Normally, we don't take test and then prepare for it.

Now, let's analyze the code. As usual, we have an inner method called *topSort* within the public method *topologicalSort*. The outer method accepts a list of tuples, which is a graph representation. The inner method take a list of unvisited vertices and a list of visited vertices. As the recursive structure continues, the list of unvisited vertices shrinks and the list of visited vertices grows. The first match clause represents completed traversal; in that case, the list of visited vertices is returned. The second match clause takes care of an unvisited vertex in the list of vertices and is done recursively until all unvisited vertices are covered. If a pre-visited vertex is found then that vertex is skipped. Otherwise, the current vertex is prepended with the result of topological sorting of its successors. This completes the topological sorting.

```scala
package com.equalinformation.dascala.scala.graphs

object TopologicalSortingApp {
  def main(args: Array[String]): Unit = {
    val myEventsList = List(("prepare_test", "take_test"),
      ("take_test", "apply"),
      ("apply", "receive_offer"),
      ("receive_offer", "join_CMU"),
      ("join_CMU", "choose_major"),
      ("choose_major", "graduate"),
      ("receive_offer", "join_MIT"),
      ("join_MIT", "choose_major"),
      ("choose_major", "graduate"))

    println(topologicalSort(myEventsList))
  }

  def topologicalSort(graph: List[(String, String)]) = {
    def topSort(vertices: List[String], visited:
      List[String]): List[String] = vertices match {
      case Nil => visited
      case x :: xs => topSort(xs,
        if(visited.contains(x)) visited
        else x :: topSort(calcSuccessorSet(x, graph),
          visited))
    }

    val (start, _) = graph.unzip
    val result = topSort(start, List())
    result
  }

  def calcSuccessorSet(vertex: String, graph: List[(String,
    String)]): List[String] = graph match {
    case Nil => Nil
    case x :: xs if (vertex == x._1) => x._2 ::
      calcSuccessorSet(vertex, xs)
    case _ :: xs => calcSuccessorSet(vertex, xs)
  }

}
```

Fig. 11.3: Topological sorting

Exercise 11.2. *Cycle Detection in Topological Sorting*

Cycles can create confusion while ordering items, in terms of precedence. So it is important to detect and handle them properly. For this exercise, return a separate list of vertices that create cycles. So your *result* type is $(List[String], List[String])$. For testing, add a tuple, (*"choose_major"*, *"join_MIT"*) or something equivalent that forms a cycle. If your program is implemented correctly, your output will look like:

```
(List(prepare_test, take_test, apply, receive_offer,
join_CMU, choose_major, join_MIT, graduate),
List(choose_major))
```

Note the second list and its content, *choose_major*.

One of the interesting applications of graphs is modeling electronic circuits. Air traffic controllers can make use of graphs of flight networks. Similarly, highway networks can be modeled with graphs for analysis and design. The other popular domains are the Internet, intranets, and the World-Wide Web (WWW). These days, social networking applications make heavy use of graph models. There are over a dozen graph-based databases. One of the state of the art graph databases is Neo4j [Neo18]. Build tools like Maven, Make, or Ant utilize precedence. For example, module A may have a dependency on module B. In this case, module B must be built before module A can be built.

Exercise 11.3. *Graph Databases Research*

Make a list of known graph-based databases by searching online. From your list, select the five most popular databases and analyze how graph theories were used while building those databases. This should give you good idea of the importance of graph-related structures and algorithms.

11.5 Dijkstra's Shortest Path Algorithm

Let's say you are a brilliant computer programmer working for one of the highest paying tech companies, in Silicon Valley, such as Google, Apple, Facebook, or Amazon. You make a lot of money and would like to travel in order to get a short break from your work. Let's assume you are attracted by the beauty of the Himalayas and have found Kathmandu as your destination. Further, let's assume that you want to spend as little as possible (even though you are traveling to one of the magnificent Himalayan cities in Nepal) for your travel to Kathmandu and invest the rest of your money so that you can travel to other destinations in the future. There are many transits that can be used to fly to Kathmandu. Also there are numerous airline services that can be combined to fly to Kathmandu from Silicon Valley using transits. In this context, it is desirable to find the most economical travel route. The most economical route can be called the shortest path, in terms of cost. A famous Dutch computer scientist, Dr. Edsger W. Dijkstra, conceived this algorithm in the late 1950s.

Now, let's first outline Dijkstra's shortest path algorithm.

1. Select a start vertex; this is very likely to come from a problem definition
2. Initialize the distance of the start vertex from the start vertex as 0
3. Initialize the distance of all other vertices from the start vertex as ∞
4. **WHILE** there is at least one unvisited vertex
   Visit the unvisited vertex with the smallest known distance from
   the start vertex
   FOR each unvisited neighbor of the current vertex
      Calculate the distance from the start vertex
      IF the calculated distance is less than the known distance
         Update the shortest distance to this vertex
         Update the previous vertex name with the current vertex name
      END IF
   Add the current vertex to the list of visited vertices
   END WHILE

Now, let's take a simple example and walk through the algorithm. We have a set of vertices $V = \{P, Q, R, S, T\}$. Vertices are connected with bidirectional edges, i.e., there are cycles present. Dijkstra's algorithm can work with cycles too. The weights of the edges are shown in the small boxes. The graph is visualized in Figure 11.4.

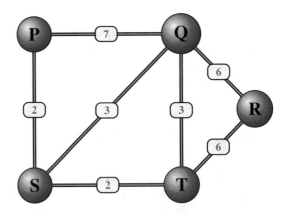

Fig. 11.4: Dijkstra'a algorithm: given problem

Now, let's walk through the algorithm stepwise:

- Step 1: Initial state: P is the starting vertex, the distance from P to P is 0, and the distance from P to all other vertices is ∞. *Visited* = [] and *Unvisited* = [P, Q, R, S, T].

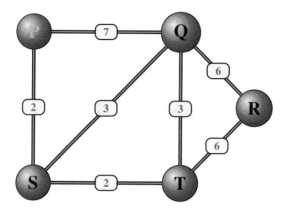

Fig. 11.5: Dijkstra'a algorithm: S1 graph

This step is visualized in Figure 11.5 and the corresponding state information is shown in Table 11.1.

Table 11.1: Dijkstra's algorithm: S1 state

Vertex	Shortest distance from P	Previous vertex
P	0	
Q	∞	
R	∞	
S	∞	
T	∞	

- Step 2: Visit P, distance is 0. Visit P's neighbors: Q and S. The distance from P to Q is 7 and the distance from P to S is 2. Since our shortest distances for all other vertices are still ∞, we can update the calculated values. *Visited* = [P] and *Unvisited* = [Q, R, S, T]. Since we visited Q and S via *P*, we enter P as the previous vertex for both.
  This step is visualized in Figure 11.6 and the corresponding state information is shown in Table 11.2.
- Step 3: The shortest known distance in the table is 2, which corresponds to vertex S. So now we visit vertex S and calculate the distance from the starting vertex P to its neighbors: Q and T. P is also the neighbor of S, but we won't visit it because we have already visited P. The calculated distance from P to Q is 5, which is less than the known shortest distance 7. Hence 7 is replaced by 5. Similarly, the

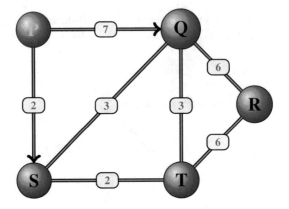

Fig. 11.6: Dijkstra'a algorithm: S2 graph

Table 11.2: Dijkstra's algorithm: S2 state

Vertex	Shortest distance from P	Previous vertex
P	0	
Q	7	P
R	∞	
S	2	P
T	∞	

shortest known distance for T is still ∞ and the calculated distance is 4. Hence
∞ is replaced by 4. This time, we visited Q via S, so the previous vertex P is
replaced by S. We visited T via S and hence the previous vertex is updated to S.
Visited = [P, S] and *Unvisited* = [Q, R, T].

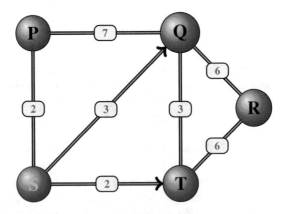

Fig. 11.7: Dijkstra'a algorithm: S3 graph

This step is visualized in Figure 11.7 and the corresponding state information is shown in Table 11.3.

Table 11.3: Dijkstra's algorithm: S3 state

Vertex	Shortest distance from P	Previous vertex
P	0	
Q	5	S
R	∞	
S	2	P
T	4	S

- Step 4: Among the unvisited vertices in the list, the vertex T has the shortest distance from starting vertex A, so we visit vertex T, in this step. It has two unvisited neighbors: Q and R. Now, distance from P to Q = distance from P to T from the state table + distance from T to Q = $4 + 3 = 7$. Similarly, the calculated distance from P to R is 10. The shortest known distance for R is still ∞, so we update it by 10. The shortest known distance for Q is 5, which is less than 7, so we don't update it. We add one more entry in the visited list, so $Visited = [P, S, T]$ and $Unvisited = [Q, R]$.

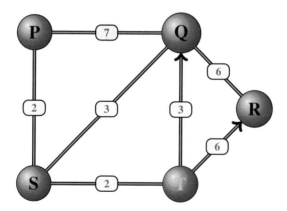

Fig. 11.8: Dijkstra'a algorithm: S4 graph

This step is visualized in Figure 11.8 and the corresponding state information is shown in Table 11.4.

- Step 5: Following the same logic, we visit Q next. It has only one unvisited neighbor, R. The calculated distance from P to R via Q = $5 + 6 = 11$, which is greater than the existing entry for R. So we don't update the shortest distance. Since the shortest distance is not updated, we don't have to update previous ver-

Table 11.4: Dijkstra's algorithm: S4 state

Vertex	Shortest distance from P	Previous vertex
P	0	
Q	5	S
R	10	T
S	2	P
T	4	S

tex. Again, we add one more entry in the visited list, so $Visited = [P, S, T, Q]$ and $Unvisited = [R]$.

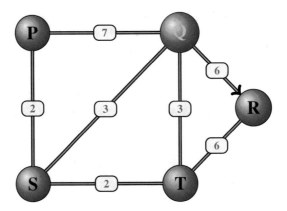

Fig. 11.9: Dijkstra'a algorithm: S5 graph

This step is visualized in Figure 11.9 and the corresponding state information is available in Table 11.5.

Table 11.5: Dijkstra's algorithm: S5 state

Vertex	Shortest distance from P	Previous vertex
P	0	
Q	5	S
R	10	T
S	2	P
T	4	S

- Step 6: Finally, we visit R as it has the shortest known distance from the starting vertex P, among unvisited vertices; it is the only unvisited vertex left. Since it doesn't have any unvisited neighbors, we only update the visited and unvisited lists. So $Visited = [P, S, T, Q, R]$ and $Unvisited = []$.

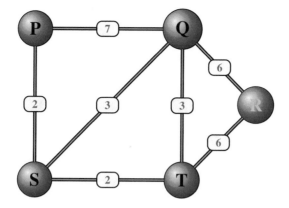

Fig. 11.10: Dijkstra'a algorithm: S6 graph

This step is visualized in Figure 11.10 and the corresponding state information is shown in Table 11.6.

Table 11.6: Dijkstra's algorithm: S6 state

Vertex	Shortest distance from P	Previous vertex
P	0	
Q	5	S
R	10	T
S	2	P
T	4	S

Now, if we look at our final state in Table 11.5, we find the shortest distance to each of the vertices from the starting vertex P. This answers many questions, because it is an exhaustive computation. In a given graph, we can find the minimum cost path from a vertex of interest to any other vertex. If we are only interested in reaching a specific destination, this greedy algorithm has a downside, i.e., it still has to do exhaustive computation. Nevertheless, Dijkstra's algorithm solves many practical problems.

Next, we will take a practical problem and solve it using a Dijkstra's algorithm implementation in Scala. Based on Google Flights data points, Figure 11.11 presents partial flight routes from San Francisco International Airport (SFO) in San Francisco, CA, USA to Tribhuvan International Airport (KTM) in Kathmandu, Nepal for 11-04-2018. The total costs are the actual costs of different routes, whereas the breakdown of each route cost is arbitrary. The costs keep changing, so arbitrary breakdown won't affect our exercise.

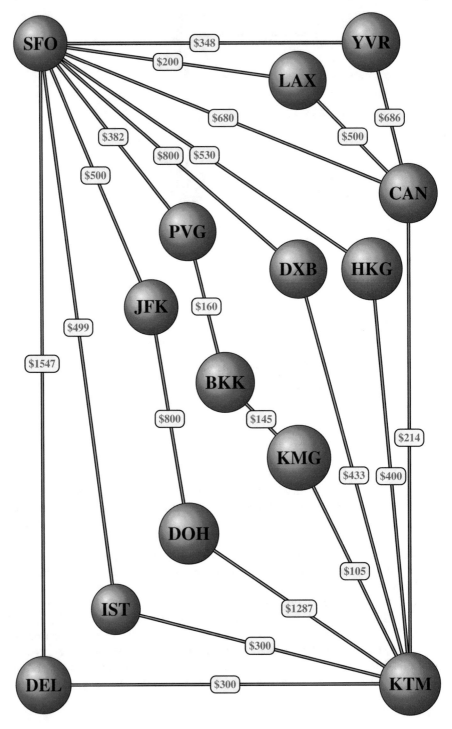

Fig. 11.11: Flight routes: San Francisco (SFO) to Kathmandu (KTM) 11-04-2018

Exercise 11.4. *State Graphs and Tables*

For the flight graph network presented in Figure 11.11, apply Dijkstra's shortest path algorithm and create all the relevant state graphs and tables.

Exercise 11.5. *Graph Building Blocks*

In order to implement the flight graph network presented in Figure 11.11 using Dijkstra's shortest path algorithm, you will need basic graph-related building blocks. Perform the following building-blocks work before implementing Dijkstra's algorithm:

1. Implement a trait called *MyGraph* with these functions: *edges*, *addEdge*, and *neighbors*. The function *edges* returns a list of vertices, the function *addEdge* returns a graph that has the currently supplied vertex, and the function *neighbors* returns a list of neighboring vertices of a given vertex.
2. Also implement a companion object called *MyGraph* with two *apply* methods. The signature of the first *apply* method is *apply[V](adjacencyList: Map[V, List[V]]): MyGraph[V]*. The signature of the second *apply* method is *apply[V]() : MyGraph[V]*.
3. Implement a class called *MyDirectedGraph* that extends the trait *MyGraph*. Here is a partial implementation:

```
class MyDirectedGraph[V](adjacencyList: Map[V,
  List[V]]) extends MyGraph[V] {
  override def vertices: List[V] =
    adjacencyList.keys.toList

  // Implement rest of the methods
}
```

4. Implement a class called *MyUnDirectedGraph* that extends *MyDirectedGraph* so that previous implementation is reused. You only need to override the *addEdge* method. Unlike the implementation in *MyDirectedGraph*, this method keeps track of the neighbors of both the source vertext and the target vertex.
5. Implement a class called *MyWeightedGraph* that takes care of edge weight. This class extends the trait *MyGraph*. Create a case class called *MyWeightedEdge* that has two constructor parameters—destination vertex and weight. In addition to overriding the trait methods, add a method called *addEdge* which takes the source vertex and an instance of *MyWeightedEdge* as its parameters so that weight of the edge added can be taken care of. Similarly, add a method called *neighborsWithWeight* that returns a list of weighted edges instead of a list of vertices.
6. Finally, write a test application to test your implementation. This test application should create a graph with some sample data. You may use your own sample data

or use the sample data provided below. In your test application, print the vertices of your graph so that you can verify that your implementation actually creates a graph correctly. Also print the neighbors of a given vertex so that you can validate the correctness of your implementation. A sample data set and a sample console output is shown below.

Sample data:

```
val myGraph = MyGraph[String]()
  .addEdge("San Francisco", "Hong Kong")
  .addEdge("Hong Kong", "Kathmandu")
  .addEdge("Kathmandu", "San Francisco")
  .addEdge("Kathmandu", "Bangkok")
  .addEdge("Bangkok", "San Francisco")
  .addEdge("Pokhara", "Bangkok")
```

Sample output for the list of vertices and neighbors of vertex "Kathmandu", respectively:

```
List(San Francisco, Bangkok, Kathmandu, Pokhara,
  Hong Kong)
List(Bangkok, San Francisco)
```

We have done the prerequisite exercise, so we are ready to implement a Dijkstra's shortest path-based solution for the problem presented in Figure 11.11. We first create a weighted graph as shown in Figure 11.12. All the edges in Figure 11.11 are represented along with their weights. *MyWeightedEdge* is a class with the following definition:

```
case class MyWeightedEdge[V](dest: V, weight: Int)
```

It takes the destination vertex and weight as its constructor parameters. One of the advantages of using a case class is that it can be used for pattern matching. The class *MyWeightedGraph* takes the adjacency list as its constructor parameter. The adjacency list is a map of vertices and a list of weighted edges. A partial class definition is shown below:

```
class MyWeightedGraph[V](adjacencyList: Map[V,
  List[MyWeightedEdge[V]]]) extends MyGraph[V] {
    // Methods implementation here
  }
```

It extends the trait *MyGraph*, which has four methods. The first method, *vertices*, returns a list of vertices. Similarly, the method *edges* returns a list of edges. The method *addEdge* takes a source vertex and a destination vertex as its input parameters. These vertices are added in the list and a corresponding graph is returned. The method *neighbors* takes a vertex and returns its neighbors as a list of vertices.

MyWeightedGraph overloads the *addEdge* method to facilitate edge-weight handling. Also it has a method called *neighborsWithWeight*, which takes a vertex and returns a list of weighted edges. Here is the definition of the trait *MyGraph*

```
trait MyGraph[V] {
    def vertices: List[V]
    def edges: List[(V,V)]
    def addEdge(a: V, b: V): MyGraph[V]
    def neighbors(x: V): List[V]
}
```

```
package com.equalinformation.dascala.scala.graphs.dijkstra_spm

object MyTravelGraph {
    val travelGraph = new MyWeightedGraph(Map("San Francisco"
      -> Nil))
      .addEdge("San Francisco", MyWeightedEdge("Vancouver",
        348))
      .addEdge("San Francisco", MyWeightedEdge("Los Angeles",
        200))
      .addEdge("San Francisco", MyWeightedEdge("Guangzhou",
        680))
      .addEdge("San Francisco", MyWeightedEdge("Hong Kong",
        530))
      .addEdge("San Francisco", MyWeightedEdge("Dubai", 800))
      .addEdge("San Francisco", MyWeightedEdge("Shanghai", 382))
      .addEdge("San Francisco", MyWeightedEdge("New York", 500))
      .addEdge("San Francisco", MyWeightedEdge("Istanbul", 499))
      .addEdge("San Francisco", MyWeightedEdge("Delhi", 1547))

      .addEdge("Vancouver", MyWeightedEdge("Guangzhou", 686))
      .addEdge("Los Angeles", MyWeightedEdge("Guangzhou", 500))
      .addEdge("Shanghai", MyWeightedEdge("Bangkok", 160))
      .addEdge("New York", MyWeightedEdge("Doha", 800))

      .addEdge("Bangkok", MyWeightedEdge("Kunming", 145))

      .addEdge("Guangzhou", MyWeightedEdge("Kathmandu", 214))
      .addEdge("Hong Kong", MyWeightedEdge("Kathmandu", 400))
      .addEdge("Kunming", MyWeightedEdge("Kathmandu", 105))
      .addEdge("Doha", MyWeightedEdge("Kathmandu", 1287))
      .addEdge("Istanbul", MyWeightedEdge("Kathmandu", 300))
      .addEdge("Delhi", MyWeightedEdge("Kathmandu", 300))

      .addEdge("Kathmandu", MyWeightedEdge("Delhi", 300))

}
```

Fig. 11.12: Travel route graph

In Figure 11.13, we present Dijkstra's shortest path implementation for the problem presented in Figure 11.11. Note that the airport codes are replaced by the corresponding cities in Figure 11.12, which are more convenient to analyze.

Now, let's discuss the code in Figure 11.13. First, we have a case class called *ShortestStep*, which has three constructor parameters—*parents*, *unVisited*, and *distances*. So we are keeping track of visited nodes, the nodes to be visited, and costs. Costs are represented by edge weights and represented by the parameter *distances* in the program. In the beginning, all distances will be ∞ except for the starting vertex, which is 0. We have a method to find the minimum, because this is what we are interested in with Dijkstra's algorithm. This method uses a *Try* structure to recover from exceptions. If a value is not found then it can return *None*. The *findMin* method is used to calculate the shortest path.

Next, we create a distances map, denoted by *distancesMap* in the program. We create it using the graph that we built in Figure 11.12. In the beginning, except for the starting node, Dijkstra's algorithm initializes all the distances to ∞, so we map them to a maximum integer value and convert the results to a map. Also we add the starting vertex map, (*"SanFrancisco" − > 0*).

Next, let's discuss the *findShortestPath* method. We supply a *ShortestStep* instance that has all the required information—visited vertices map, unvisited vertices, and distances map. It is a recursive method and we start by finding minimum in the *ShortStep* and assign that to a tuple containing vertex and current distance. Next, we recompute distances for all the neighbors of the current node that we are visiting. We do that by getting all the neighbors of the current node being processed. And we only collect such neighbors whose distance from the starting node is greater than the sum of the current node's distance and weight of edge from the current node to this neighbor. If there is such a node then we replace the distance of this neighbor with *currentDist + w*, because this is the new shortest distance from the starting node. Next, we create the parents map *newParents* to take care of newly created or changed distances. If there is any node whose distance has changed then that node's new parent is the current node being visited. Then we make a recursive call in which the current parents are replaced by new parents, the current node being processed is taken out of the unvisited list, and the distances are replaced by the new distances. Lastly, either we get the recursive step or the stopping condition using *getOrElse*. When there are no more nodes to visit we reach a stopping step. In that case, we return the step unmodified.

The method *extractShortestPaths* extracts the shortest paths so that we can print them for manual validation. It takes a vertex whose shortest path we are interested in and then its parents map. It returns a list of vertices that we need to visit in order to get to this vertex. It gets a parent node to this node and prepends that to the list. It does it recursively to get the parent of a parent and so on until there are no more parents left. When no more parent vertices are left it returns the list of vertices accumulated so far, which gives the shortest path to the vertex parameterized to this method.

In the *main* method, we write a helper function *spResult* that helps us to print the shortest path. So we invoke the *shortestPath* method which takes *ShortStep* as its parameter. For *ShortStep*, we supply an empty map for *parents* as there are no parents initially. We pass all the vertices as unvisited, which is true initially. The third parameter gets *distanceMap*, in which all the distances are initialized with the maximum integer value, as ∞ cannot be processed, along with the starting vertex being initialized to 0. Next, we print all the distances from *spResult*, which gives us the minimum cost of flight to that airport. In the last LOC, we print the shortest path for each airport in the flight route graph presented in Figure 11.11. We achieve this by traversing each vertex in *travelGraph*. For each vertex traversed, we extract the shortest path by passing that vertex and parents from *spResult* to the method *extractShortestPaths*. This completes our discussion of the solution presented in Figure 11.13. The console output is shown below.

```
Map(San Francisco -> 0, Shanghai -> 382,
  Bangkok -> 542, Kathmandu -> 792, Doha -> 1300,
  Delhi -> 1092, Los Angeles -> 200, New York -> 500,
  Hong Kong -> 530, Istanbul -> 499,
  Vancouver -> 348, Kunming -> 687, Guangzhou -> 680)
List(San Francisco)
List(San Francisco, Shanghai)
List(San Francisco, Shanghai, Bangkok)
List(San Francisco, Shanghai, Bangkok, Kunming,
  Kathmandu)
List(San Francisco, New York, Doha)
List(San Francisco, Shanghai, Bangkok, Kunming,
  Kathmandu, Delhi)
List(San Francisco, Los Angeles)
List(San Francisco, New York)
List(San Francisco, Hong Kong)
List(San Francisco, Istanbul)
List(San Francisco, Vancouver)
List(San Francisco, Shanghai, Bangkok, Kunming)
List(San Francisco, Guangzhou)
```

Exercise 11.6. *Dijkstra's Shortest Path with Multi-Weight Edges and Weighted Vertices*

The flight network presented in Figure 11.11 has an additional weight associated with each edge, which is flight time. Every vertex other than SFO and KTM has an associated weight, which is layover. Now, we have time as well as cost coming into the picture. Outline the solution steps. Examine whether Dijkstra's shortest path algorithm (SPM) can still be applied. If it can be applied, create relevant state graphs and tables. Also provide a corresponding Scala implementation. If Dijkstra's SPM cannot be applied, provide your reasoning.

```
package com.equalinformation.dascala.scala.graphs.dijkstra_spm
import com.equalinformation.dascala.scala.graphs.dijkstra_spm
  .MyTravelGraph.travelGraph

import scala.util.Try

case class ShortestStep(parents: Map[String, String],
   unVisited: Set[String],
   distances: Map[String, Int]) {
   def findMin(): Option[(String, Int)] =
      Try(unVisited.minBy(x => distances(x))).toOption.map(x =>
        (x, distances(x)))
}

object MyTravelDijkstraShortestPathApp {
   def main(args: Array[String]): Unit = {
      val spResult = findShortestPath(ShortestStep(Map(),
        travelGraph.vertices.toSet, distancesMap))
      println(spResult.distances)
      travelGraph.vertices.foreach(x =>
        println(extractShortestPaths(x,
        spResult.parents).reverse))
   }

   val distancesMap = travelGraph.vertices.map(_ ->
     Int.MaxValue).toMap + ("San Francisco" -> 0)

   def findShortestPath(step: ShortestStep): ShortestStep = {
      step.findMin().map {
         case (x, currentDist) => {
            val newDists = travelGraph.neighborsWithWeight(x)
              .collect {
              case MyWeightedEdge(y, w) if step.distances
                .get(y).exists(_ > currentDist + w) =>
                y -> (currentDist + w)
            }

            val newParents = newDists.map {
               case (y, _) => y -> x
            }

            findShortestPath(ShortestStep(step.parents ++
              newParents, step.unVisited - x, step.distances ++
              newDists))
         }

      }.getOrElse(step)

   }

   def extractShortestPaths(vertex: String, parents:
     Map[String, String]): List[String] = parents.get(vertex)
     .map(x => vertex +: extractShortestPaths(x, parents))
     .getOrElse(List(vertex))

}
```

Fig. 11.13: Dijkstra's shortest path implementation for travel route graph

Appendix A
Solutions for Selected Exercises

A.1 Chapter 3

- Solution for Exercise 3.1:

```
package com.equalinformation.dascala.scala.arrays

object MethodLengthApp {
  def main(args: Array[String]): Unit = {
    println(calcLength(Array('a', 'e', 'i', 'o', 'u', '\0')))
  }

  def calcLength(item: Array[Char]): Int = {
    var count = 0
    while(item(count) != '\0') {
      count += 1
    }

    count
  }
}
```

The solution presented above iterates through each element of the input character array and hence it has time complexity of $O(n)$.

- Solution for Exercise 3.3
  One of the array-oriented databases that has both industrial as well as academic research aspects is SciDB [Sci18] [CMMK+18]. SciDB has a consortium of distributed research and development teams located at MIT, Microsoft, Brown University, The University of Wisconsin-Madison, etc. It is an open-source, array-oriented, declarative, shared-nothing, and extensible database. The high-level architectural components include SciDB Application, Language Specific UI, Run-time Supervisor, Query Interface and Parser, Plan Generator, and Storage Layer.

© Springer Nature Switzerland AG 2019
B. P. Upadhyaya, *Data Structures and Algorithms with Scala*, Undergraduate Topics in Computer Science, https://doi.org/10.1007/978-3-030-12561-5

The storage layer is a multi-node structure and each node consists of a Local Executor and Storage Manager. A typical query execution request flows from SciDB Application to Storage Layer.

The data model consists of nested, multidimensional arrays as first-class citizens. It has basic data types and allows user-defined data types as well. The storage model supports array partitioning, with co-location of values that are related to adaptive chunking, dense packing, and compression. On-disk representations include dense arrays and sparse arrays. Dense arrays are extremely compact. Also the model allows co-location of nested arrays with reference to the parent array. In terms of redundancy, it allows array replication and chunking with overlapping that enables parallel processing.

As far as operators are concerned, SciDB supports an Array-Oriented Query Language (AQL). There are three types of operators—structural (add dimension, concatenate, etc.), content-dependent (filter, select, etc.), and structural and content-dependent (joins). There are generic operators to scatter and gather array chunks and values, in distributed environments. A typical AQL statement looks like:

```
CREATE ARRAY MyArray
    < A: integer NULLS,
      B: double,
      C: USER_DEFINED_TYPE >
    [ I=0:999999, 10000, 100, J=0:999999, 10000,
     100 ]
    PARTITION OVER ( Node1, Node2, Node3 )
    USING block_cyclic();
```

In this query, the attribute names are A, B, and C; I and J are index names; chunk size is 10,000 and overlap is defined as 100. Note that the content inside a pair of square brackets looks like a loop. We had a similar structure in our matrix multiplication application presented in Figure 3.1.

Research has shown that the array approach has many advantages for big data, including data partitioning convenience to allow both parallel and sequential processing, direct offsetting and omission of index attributes, and efficient as well as convenient multi-dimensional representation and processing. Also, benchmarking has shown that the array approach performs better than the traditional RDBMS style of representation and processing of data [CMMK+18].

A.2 Chapter 4

- Solution for Exercise 4.2:
  First, using *fold*,

```
scala> myNumList.fold(0) { (acc, x) => acc + x }
res6: Int = 12
```

```
scala> myNumList.fold(0)(_ + _)
res7: Int = 12
```

fold doesn't have a particular order, as opposed to *foldLeft* and *foldRight*. Here is one possible sequence of steps for *fold*.

```
op(acc = 0, x = 2), op(acc = 0, x = 4);
2, op(acc = 4, x = 6)
   or, 2, op(op(acc = 0, x = 4), 6);
op(acc = 2, x = 10)
   or, op(acc = 2, op(op(acc = 0, x = 4), 6));
```

Now, using *foldLeft*,

```
scala> val myNumList: List[Int] = List(2,4,6)
myNumList: List[Int] = List(2, 4, 6)

scala> myNumList.foldLeft(0) {
  (acc, x) => acc + x }
res0: Int = 12

scala> myNumList.foldLeft(3) {
  (acc, x) => acc + x }
res1: Int = 15

scala> myNumList.foldLeft(0)(_ + _)
res2: Int = 12

scala> myNumList.foldLeft(3)(_ + _)
res3: Int = 15
```

The *foldLeft* function in our code snippet takes two arguments—an initial value and a pre-defined combining operation *op* that takes two arguments: the accumulated value *acc* and the current value. It processes the traversable list in this case from left to right. Note that the code snippet above presents two different solutions with different initial values to give an idea of how an initial value is processed.

Here is how *op* is applied in steps:

```
op(acc = 0, x = 2) // 2;
op(acc = 2, x = 4) // 6
   or, op(op(acc = 0, x = 2), 4);
op(acc = 6, x = 6) // 12,
   or, op(op(op(acc = 0, x = 2), 4), 6);
```

Now, using *foldRight*, we get the same result but the internal computational steps are different.

```
scala> myNumList.foldRight(0) {
 (acc, x) => acc + x }
res4: Int = 12

scala> myNumList.foldRight(0)(_ + _)
res5: Int = 12
```

In this case, the detailed steps are:

```
op(acc = 0, x = 6) // 6;
op(acc = 6, x = 4) // 10
  or, op(op(acc = 0, x = 6), 4);
op(acc = 10, x = 2)  // 12
  or, op(op(op(acc = 0, x = 6), 4), 2);
```

- Solution for Exercise 4.3

  1. Getting the value for a given integer index:

```
scala> val myNumList: List[Int] = List(2,4,6)
myNumList: List[Int] = List(2, 4, 6)

scala> def get[A](list: List[A], index: Int): A =
 | list.tail.foldLeft(list.head, 0) {
 | (x, y) => if(x._2 == index) x else (y, x._2 +1)
 | } match {
 | case (result, ind) if (index == ind) => result
 | case _ => throw new Exception("Incorrect index")
 | }
get: [A](list: List[A], index: Int)A

scala> get(myNumList, 0)
res12: Int = 2

scala> get(myNumList, 2)
res13: Int = 6

scala> get(myNumList, 3)
java.lang.Exception: Incorrect index
at .get(<console>:15)
... 33 elided
```

  2. Calculating the average of values:

```
scala> val myNewNumList = List(2.0, 4.0, 6.0)
myNewNumList: List[Double] = List(2.0, 4.0, 6.0)

scala> def calcAverage(list: List[Double]):
 | Double = list match {
```

```
| case head :: tail => tail.foldLeft(head, 1.0) {
| (x, y) =>
| ((x._1 * x._2 + y)/(x._2 + 1.0), x._2 + 1.0)
| }._1
| case Nil => throw new Exception("Not a Number")
| }
calcAverage: (list: List[Double])Double

scala> calcAverage(myNewNumList)
res16: Double = 4.0
```

3. Reversing a given list:

```
scala> def rev[A](list: List[A]): List[A] =
   list.foldLeft(List[A]()) { (x, y) => y :: x}
rev: [A](list: List[A])List[A]

scala> rev(myNumList)
res11: List[Int] = List(6, 4, 2)
```

4. Getting the last element of a list using *foldLeft*:

```
scala> def getLast[A](list: List[A]): A =
   list.foldLeft[A](list.head) { (_, x) => x }
getLast: [A](list: List[A])A

scala> getLast(myNumList)
res9: Int = 6
```

5. Calculating the length of a list using *foldLeft*:

```
scala> def listLength(list: List[Any]): Int =
   list.foldLeft(0) { (count, _) => count + 1}
listLength: (list: List[Any])Int

scala> listLength(myNumList)
res8: Int = 3
```

A.3 Chapter 5

• Solution for Problem 5.2:

```scala
package com.equalinformation.dascala.scala.stacks

class MyStackGen(maxSize: Int) {
   private var stackBox = new Array[Any](maxSize)
   private var top = -1

   def push(data: Any): Unit = {
      top += 1
      stackBox(top) = data
   }

   def pop(): Any = {
      val popData = stackBox(top)
      top -= 1
      popData
   }

   def peek(): Any = {
      stackBox(top)
   }

   def isEmpty(): Boolean = {
      return (top == -1)
   }

   def isFull(): Boolean = {
      return (top == maxSize - 1)
   }
}

object WordReverseImpApp {
   def main(args: Array[String]): Unit = {
      print("Enter a word: ")
      val inputWord = scala.io.StdIn.readLine().toString
      val myReverser = new Reverser(inputWord)

      println("Reverse word: "+myReverser.reverse)
   }
}
```

A.4 Chapter 6

- Solution for Problem 6.2:

```
package com.equalinformation.dascala.scala.queues

case class FQueueGen(out: List[Any], in: List[Any]) {
   def check(): Boolean = (out, in) match {
      case (Nil, x :: xs) => false
      case _ => true
   }

   require(check, "Didn't satisfy invariant")
}

object FunctQueueGenApp {
   def main(args: Array[String]): Unit = {
      val myQueue = insert("apple", insert("banana",
         insert("mango", FQueueGen(Nil, Nil))))
      println(remove(remove(myQueue)._2))
   }

   def insert(data: Any, queue: FQueueGen): FQueueGen = {
      val newIn = data :: queue.in
      queue.out match {
         case Nil => FQueueGen(newIn.reverse, Nil)
         case _ => queue.copy(in = newIn)
      }
   }

   def remove(queue: FQueueGen): (Any, FQueueGen) = {
      queue.out match {
         case Nil => throw new
            IllegalArgumentException("Queue is empty!")
         case x :: Nil => (x, queue.copy(out =
            queue.in.reverse, Nil))
         case y :: ys => (y, queue.copy(out = ys))
      }
   }

}
```

A.5 Chapter 8

- Solution for Exercise 8.1: see Figure A.1.
- Solution for Exercise 8.2: see Figure A.2.
- Solution for Exercise 8.3: see Figure A.3.
- Solution for Exercise 8.4: see Figure A.4.

```scala
package com.equalinformation.dascala.scala.bin_trees

object CompareBinTreesApp {
   def main(args: Array[String]): Unit = {
      val binTree1 = createTree(List(1,2,3,4,5))
      val binTree2 = createTree(List(2,1,3,4,5))
      println(equal(binTree1, binTree2))
   }

   def equal[A](binTree1: BinaryTree[A], binTree2:
     BinaryTree[A]): Boolean = (binTree1, binTree2) match {
     case (Leaf, Leaf) => true
     case (Branch(v1, lb1, rb1), Branch(v2, lb2, rb2)) if v1
       == v2 => equal(lb1, lb2) && equal(rb1, rb2)
     case _ => false
   }

   def createTree[A](list: List[A]): BinaryTree[A] =
     list match {
     case Nil => Leaf
     case x :: xs => {
        val halfLength = xs.length / 2
        Branch(x, createTree(xs.take(halfLength)),
          createTree(xs.drop(halfLength)))
     }
   }
}
```

Fig. A.1: Binary tree equality check

```scala
package com.equalinformation.dascala.scala.bin_trees

object CompleteBinaryTreeApp {
   def main(args: Array[String]): Unit = {
      val myCompleteBinTree = createCompleteBinaryTree(2, 3);
      println(myCompleteBinTree)
   }

   def createCompleteBinaryTree(value: Int, depth: Int):
     BinaryTree[Int] =
     if(depth == 0) Leaf
     else Branch(value, createCompleteBinaryTree(2 * value,
       depth - 1), createCompleteBinaryTree(2 * value + 1,
       depth -1))
}
```

Fig. A.2: Complete binary tree

```scala
package com.equalinformation.dascala.scala.bin_trees

object BinTreeFlippingApp {
  def main(args: Array[String]): Unit = {
    val myList = List(1,2,3,4,5,6)
    val myBinTree = createTree(myList)
    println(myBinTree)
    println(flip(myBinTree))
  }

  def flip[A](binTree: BinaryTree[A]): BinaryTree[A] =
    binTree match {
      case Leaf => Leaf
      case Branch(value, leftBranch, rightBranch) =>
        Branch(value, flip(rightBranch), flip(leftBranch))
    }

  def createTree[A](list: List[A]): BinaryTree[A] =
    list match {
      case Nil => Leaf
      case x :: xs => {
        val halfLength = xs.length / 2
        Branch(x, createTree(xs.take(halfLength)),
          createTree(xs.drop(halfLength)))
      }
    }

}
```

Fig. A.3: Binary tree flipping

```scala
package com.equalinformation.dascala.scala.bin_trees

object BinTreeFlipCheckApp {
    def main(args: Array[String]): Unit = {
        val myList = List(1,2,3,4,5,6)
        val myBinTree = createTree(myList)
        val myBinTreeFlipped = flip(myBinTree)
        println(myBinTree)
        println(myBinTreeFlipped)
        println(flipEqual(myBinTree, myBinTreeFlipped))
    }

    def flipEqual[A](binTree1: BinaryTree[A], binTree2:
      BinaryTree[A]): Boolean = (binTree1, binTree2) match {
        case (Leaf, Leaf) => true
        case (Branch(value1, leftBranch1, rightBranch1),
            Branch(value2, leftBranch2, rightBranch2)) if
            value1 == value2 => flipEqual(leftBranch1,
            rightBranch2) && flipEqual(leftBranch2, rightBranch1)
        case _ => false
    }

    def createTree[A](list: List[A]): BinaryTree[A] =
      list match {
        case Nil => Leaf
        case x :: xs => {
            val halfLength = xs.length / 2
            Branch(x, createTree(xs.take(halfLength)),
              createTree(xs.drop(halfLength)))
        }
    }

    def flip[A](binTree: BinaryTree[A]): BinaryTree[A] =
      binTree match {
        case Leaf => Leaf
        case Branch(value, leftBranch, rightBranch) =>
          Branch(value, flip(rightBranch), flip(leftBranch))
    }
}
```

Fig. A.4: Binary tree flipped equality check

A.6 Chapter 9

- Solution for Exercise 9.1: see Figure A.5.

```scala
package com.equalinformation.dascala.scala.sorting

object BubbleSortDescApp {
  def main(args: Array[String]): Unit = {
    println(bubbleSortDesc(List(3,1,6,8,2)))
    println(bubbleSortDesc(List("z", "c", "a", "b")))
  }

  def bubbleSortDesc[T <% Ordered[T]](myData: List[T]):
    List[T] = myData match {
    case Nil => Nil
    case _ => {
      val (min, remainingData) = calcMin(myData)
      bubbleSortDesc(remainingData) ::: List(min)
    }
  }

  def calcMin[T <% Ordered[T]](myData: List[T]): (T,
    List[T]) = myData match {
    case (Nil) => (null.asInstanceOf[T], Nil)
    case (head :: Nil) => (head, Nil)
    case (head :: tail) => {
      val (tailMin, tailRemaining) = calcMin(tail)
      if (tailMin <= head) (tailMin, head :: tailRemaining)
      else (head, tailMin :: tailRemaining)
    }
  }
}
```

Fig. A.5: Bubble sort: descending

- Solution for Exercise 9.3: see Figure A.6.
- Solution for Exercise 9.5: see Figure A.7.
- Solution for Exercise 9.7: see Figure A.8.
- Solution for Exercise 9.9: see Figure A.9.

```scala
package com.equalinformation.dascala.scala.sorting

object SelectionSortDescApp {
  def main(args: Array[String]): Unit = {
    println(selectionSortDesc(List(5,3,2,8,7)))
    println(selectionSortDesc(List("k","d","c","a","q")))
  }

  def selectionSortDesc[T <% Ordered[T]](myData:
    List[T]): List[T] = myData match {
    case Nil => Nil
    case head :: Nil => List(head)
    case head :: tail => {
      val maxElem = tail.max
      val indexOfMaxElem = tail.indexOf(maxElem)
      if(head >= maxElem) {
        head :: selectionSortDesc(tail)
      } else {
        val (tailHalf1, tailHalf2) =
          tail.splitAt(indexOfMaxElem)
        tailHalf2.head :: selectionSortDesc(tailHalf1 :::
          head :: tailHalf2.tail)
      }
    }
  }
}
```

Fig. A.6: Selection sort: descending

```scala
package com.equalinformation.dascala.scala.sorting

object InsertionSortDescApp {
  def main(args: Array[String]): Unit = {
    println(insertionSortDesc(List(15,10,33,11)))
    println(insertionSortDesc(List("banana","apple",
      "mango")))
  }

  def insertionSortDesc[T <% Ordered[T]](myData: List[T]):
    List[T] = {
    if (myData == Nil) {
      myData
    } else {
      val head :: tail = myData
      val temp = insertionSortDesc(tail)
      insertElementDesc(head, temp)
    }
  }

  def insertElementDesc[T <% Ordered[T]](elem: T,
    sortedSubList: List[T]): List[T] = {
    if(sortedSubList == Nil) {
      return elem :: sortedSubList
    } else {
      val head :: tail = sortedSubList
      if (head >= elem) {
        head :: insertElementDesc(elem, tail)
      } else {
        elem :: sortedSubList
      }
    }
  }
}
```

Fig. A.7: Insertion sort: descending

```scala
package com.equalinformation.dascala.scala.sorting

object MergeSortDescApp {
  def main(args: Array[String]): Unit = {
    println(mergeSortDesc(List(5,6,2,3,1)))
    println(mergeSortDesc(List("cat", "put", "bag")))
  }

  def mergeSortDesc[T <% Ordered[T]](myData: List[T]):
    List[T] = {
    if( myData == Nil || myData.tail == Nil) {
      return myData
    }

    val (myDataSplit1, myDataSplit2) = split(myData)
    val sortedSL1 = mergeSortDesc(myDataSplit1)
    val sortedSL2 = mergeSortDesc(myDataSplit2)
    mergeDesc(sortedSL1, sortedSL2)
  }

  def mergeDesc[T <% Ordered[T]](sortedSubList1: List[T],
    sortedSubList2: List[T]): List[T] = (sortedSubList1,
    sortedSubList2) match {
    case (sortedSubList1, Nil) => sortedSubList1
    case (Nil, sortedSubList2) => sortedSubList2
    case (x1 :: y1, x2 :: y2) =>
      if (x1 < x2) x2 :: mergeDesc(sortedSubList1, y2)
      else x1 :: mergeDesc(y1, sortedSubList2)
  }

  def split[T <% Ordered[T]](myData: List[T]): (List[T],
    List[T]) = {
    if (myData == Nil) {
      return (Nil, Nil)
    }

    val headOfmyData = myData.head
    val tailOfmyData = myData.tail
    if(tailOfmyData == Nil) {
      return (headOfmyData :: Nil, Nil)
    }
    val headOfTailOfmyData = tailOfmyData.head
    val tailOfTailOfmyData = tailOfmyData.tail
    val (tailOfTailOfmyDataSplit1, tailOfTailOfmyDataSplit2)
      = split(tailOfTailOfmyData)
    return (headOfmyData :: tailOfTailOfmyDataSplit1,
      headOfTailOfmyData :: tailOfTailOfmyDataSplit2)
  }
}
```

Fig. A.8: Merge sort: descending

```scala
package com.equalinformation.dascala.scala.sorting

object QuickSortDesc {
   def main(args: Array[String]): Unit = {
      println(quickSortDesc(List(5,2,1,6,7)))
      println(quickSortDesc(List("grape","apple","apricot")))
   }

   def quickSortDesc[T <% Ordered[T]](myData:
     List[T]): List[T] = myData match {
      case Nil => Nil
      case head :: Nil => List(head)
      case head :: tail => {
         val (p1, p2) = partitionDesc(head, tail, Nil, Nil)
         val leftToPivot = quickSortDesc(p1)
         val rightToPivot = quickSortDesc(p2)
         val temp = head :: rightToPivot
         return leftToPivot ++ temp
      }
   }

   def partitionDesc[T <% Ordered[T]](pivot: T, myData:
     List[T], p1: List[T], p2: List[T]): (List[T], List[T]) =
     myData match {
      case Nil => (p1, p2)
      case head :: tail =>
         if (head > pivot) partitionDesc(pivot, tail, head ::
           p1, p2)
         else partitionDesc(pivot, tail, p1, head :: p2)
   }

}
```

Fig. A.9: Quick sort: descending

A.7 Chapter 10

- Solution for Exercise 10.1:

```
package com.equalinformation.dascala.scala.searching

object NaiveSubstringSearchImperativeApp {
   def main(args: Array[String]): Unit = {
      val myData1 = "This is an imperative implementation."
      val myWords1 = "imperative"
      println(naiveSubstringSearchImperative(myWords1,
        myData1))
   }

   def naiveSubstringSearchImperative(myWords: String,
     myData:String): Int = {
     var index = -1
     for(i <- 0 to myData.length - myWords.length if
       index == -1) {
       var j = 0

       while(j < myWords.length && myData(i + j) ==
         myWords(j)) {
           j += 1
       }

       if (j == myWords.length) {
           index = i
       }
     }

     index
   }

}
```

A.8 Chapter 11

- Solution for Exercise 11.2: see Figure A.10.
- Solution for Exercise 11.5: see Figure A.11 to Figure A.15.

```scala
package com.equalinformation.dascala.scala.graphs

object TopologicalSortCycleDetectionApp {
    def main(args: Array[String]): Unit = {
        val myEventsList = List(("prepare_test", "take_test"),
          ("take_test", "apply"),
          ("apply", "receive_offer"),
          ("receive_offer", "join_CMU"),
          ("join_CMU", "choose_major"),
          ("choose_major", "graduate"),
          ("receive_offer", "join_MIT"),
          ("join_MIT", "choose_major"),
          ("choose_major", "graduate"),
          ("choose_major", "join_MIT"))

        println(topoSortDetectCycle(myEventsList))
    }

    def topoSortDetectCycle(graph: List[(String, String)]) = {
        def topoSort(vertices: List[String], path: List[String],
          vc: (List[String], List[String])): (List[String],
          List[String]) = vertices match {
          case Nil => vc
          case x :: xs => {
             val (visited, cycle) = vc
             topoSort(xs, path,
                if (path.contains(x)) (visited, x :: cycle)
                else if (visited.contains(x)) vc
                else addToVisitedTL(x, topoSort(
                   calcSuccessorSet(x, graph), x :: path, vc))
             )
          }
        }

        val (start, _) = graph.unzip
        val result = topoSort(start, List(), (List(), List()))
        result
    }

    def calcSuccessorSet(vertex: String, graph: List[(String,
      String)]): List[String] = graph match {
      case Nil => Nil
      case x :: xs if (vertex == x._1) => x._2 ::
        calcSuccessorSet(vertex, xs)
      case _ :: xs => calcSuccessorSet(vertex, xs)
    }

    def addToVisitedTL(value: String, vc: (List[String],
      List[String])) = (value :: vc._1, vc._2)

}
```

Fig. A.10: Topological sorting and cycle detection

1. `package com.equalinformation.dascala.scala.graphs.dijkstra_spm`

```scala
trait MyGraph[V] {
   def vertices: List[V]
   def edges: List[(V,V)]
   def addEdge(a: V, b: V): MyGraph[V]
   def neighbors(x: V): List[V]
}

object MyGraph {
   def apply[V](adjacencyList: Map[V, List[V]]): MyGraph[V] =
      new MyDirectedGraph(adjacencyList)
   def apply[V](): MyGraph[V] = new MyDirectedGraph(Map[V,
      List[V]]())
}
```

Fig. A.11: A typical graph trait with singleton object

2. `package com.equalinformation.dascala.scala.graphs.dijkstra_spm`

```scala
class MyDirectedGraph[V](adjacencyList: Map[V, List[V]])
  extends MyGraph[V] {
  override def vertices: List[V] = adjacencyList.keys.toList

  override def edges: List[(V, V)] = adjacencyList.flatMap {
    case (v, neighbors) => neighbors.map(x =>(v,x))
  }.toList

  override def addEdge(a: V, b: V): MyDirectedGraph[V] = {
    val aNeighbors = b +: neighbors(a)
    new MyDirectedGraph(adjacencyList + (a -> aNeighbors))
  }

  override def neighbors(x: V): List[V] =
    adjacencyList.getOrElse(x, Nil)
}
```

Fig. A.12: A typical directed graph implementation

3. `package com.equalinformation.dascala.scala.graphs.dijkstra_spm`

```scala
class MyUndirectedGraph[V](adjacencyList: Map[V, List[V]])
  extends MyDirectedGraph[V](adjacencyList) {
  override def addEdge(a: V, b: V): MyUndirectedGraph[V] = {
    val aNeighbors = b +: neighbors(a)
    val bNeighbors = a +: neighbors(b)
    new MyUndirectedGraph(adjacencyList + (a -> aNeighbors,
      b -> bNeighbors))
  }
}
```

Fig. A.13: A typical undirected graph implementation

4.
```scala
package com.equalinformation.dascala.scala.graphs.dijkstra_spm

case class MyWeightedEdge[V](dest: V, weight: Int)

class MyWeightedGraph[V](adjacencyList: Map[V,
  List[MyWeightedEdge[V]]]) extends MyGraph[V] {
    override def vertices: List[V] = adjacencyList.keys.toList

    override def edges: List[(V, V)] = adjacencyList.flatMap {
      case (v, edgeList) => edgeList.map(e => v -> e.dest)
    }.toList

    def addEdge(a: V, weightedEdge: MyWeightedEdge[V]):
      MyWeightedGraph[V] = {
      val aNeighbors = weightedEdge +:
        adjacencyList.getOrElse(a, Nil)
      new MyWeightedGraph(adjacencyList + (a -> aNeighbors))
    }

    override def addEdge(a: V, b: V): MyWeightedGraph[V] =
      addEdge(a, new MyWeightedEdge(b, weight = 0))

    override def neighbors(x: V): List[V] =
      adjacencyList.getOrElse(x, Nil).map(_.dest)

    def neighborsWithWeight(x: V): List[MyWeightedEdge[V]] =
      adjacencyList.getOrElse(x, Nil).toList
}
```

Fig. A.14: A typical weighted graph implementation

5.
```scala
package com.equalinformation.dascala.scala.graphs.dijkstra_spm

object MyGraphApp {
    def main(args: Array[String]): Unit = {
      val myGraph = MyGraph[String]()
        .addEdge("San Francisco", "Hong Kong")
        .addEdge("Hong Kong", "Kathmandu")
        .addEdge("Kathmandu", "San Francisco")
        .addEdge("Kathmandu", "Bangkok")
        .addEdge("Bangkok", "San Francisco")
        .addEdge("Pokhara", "Bangkok")

      println(myGraph.vertices)
      println(myGraph.neighbors("Kathmandu"))
    }

}
```

Fig. A.15: A typical graph test application

Appendix B
Review of Discrete Mathematical Topics

In this appendix, we present a summary of discrete topics of interest from data structures and algorithms point of view.

B.1 Logarithms

In this section, we list information related to logarithms.

- *log* is used to represent logarithms to base 10, called common logarithms. *Definition: The function that takes any positive number x as input and returns the exponent to which the base 10 must be raised to obtain x; it is represented by $log(x)$.* Example: $log(100) = log_{10}(100) = log_{10}(10^2) = 2$.
- *lg* is used to represent logarithms to base 2, called binary logarithms. *Definition: The function that takes any positive number x as input and returns the exponent to which the base 2 must be raised to obtain x; it is represented by $lg(x)$.* Example: $lg(32) = log_2(32) = log_2(2^5) = 5$.
- *ln* is used to denote logarithms to base e, called natural logarithms. *Definition: The function that takes any positive number x as input and returns the exponent to which the base e must be raised to obtain x; it is represented by $ln(x)$. e denotes the number 2.71828...* Example: $ln(1) = log_{2.71828...}(1) = log_{2.71828}(e^0) = 0$. In addition, $ln(e) = log_{2.71828...}(e) = log_{2.71828...}(e^1) = 1$.
- $ln(x)$ and e^x are inverse functions. So, if $e^x = y$ then $x = ln(y)$, which implies $e^{ln(y)} = y$. Also, $x = ln(e^x)$.
- You might have already noticed: $log \Leftrightarrow log_{10}$, $lg \Leftrightarrow log_2$, and $ln \Leftrightarrow log_{2.71828...}$. Note that some software engineering authors approximate lg with log. Mathematically, they are not same but it might make sense to approximate in practice if the difference between the two doesn't alter the analysis results.
- Generalizing:

   1. $log_b(b^x) = x$
   2. $log_b(uv) = log_b(u) + log_b(v)$

© Springer Nature Switzerland AG 2019
B. P. Upadhyaya, *Data Structures and Algorithms with Scala*, Undergraduate
Topics in Computer Science, https://doi.org/10.1007/978-3-030-12561-5

3. $log_b\left(\frac{u}{v}\right) = log_b(u) - log_b(v)$

4. $log_b(u^v) = v \, log_b(u)$

5. $log_b(x) = \frac{log_c(x)}{log_c(b)} = (log_b(c))(log_c(x))$

B.2 Floor and Ceiling Functions

- For a real number x, the floor function returns the greatest integer that is less than x. It is denoted by $\lfloor x \rfloor$.
- For a real number x, the ceiling function returns the smallest integer that is greater than x. It is denoted by $\lceil x \rceil$.

B.3 Asymptotic Notations

Asymptotic notations allow us to analyze an algorithm's running time by identifying its behavior as a function of its input; input size can increase or decrease. Most of the time, we are interested in increasing input size, as that is the one that causes problems, in terms of scaling. In software engineering practice, many engineers report software systems being slow when input size increases significantly. The word "significantly" is relative to the available CPU, memory, disk, and network bandwidth. That's why we use asymptotic notations, which allow us to express complexities in relative terms so that we can choose one algorithm over another.

In Table B.1, we present notations, meanings, and relations.

Table B.1: Asymptotic notations and their meanings

Notations	Analogy	Imprecise Meaning
$f(n) = O(g(n))$	$\leq$	$f(n)$ grows more slowly or at the same rate as $g(n)$.
$f(n) = o(g(n))$	$<$	$f(n)$ grows more slowly than $g(n)$.
$f(n) = \Omega(g(n))$	$\geq$	$f(n)$ grows faster or at the same rate as $g(n)$.
$f(n) = \omega(g(n))$	$>$	$f(n)$ grows faster than $g(n)$.
$f(n) = \theta(g(n))$	$=$	$f(n)$ grows at the same rate as $g(n)$.

Now let's use set theoretic notations. As sets of functions, the following relations hold true.

- $o(g) \subseteq O(g)$
- $\omega(g) \subseteq \Omega(g)$
- $\theta(g) = O(g) \cap \Omega(g)$

We have used big O notation extensively in this book. This is true for many practitioner-oriented books because knowing the upper bound helps practitioners to save systems from crashing or performing too slowly. Also this can be a good basis for algorithmic selection. Knowing complexity in terms of θ notation is even better, but might be a bit more involved. Summarized in Table B.1, big O notation is a symbolism that is widely used in computer science, complexity theory, and mathematics to formally describe how fast a function grows or declines. In terms of notations, for a problem of size n, a constant-time algorithm is "order 1", denoted by $O(1)$. A linear-time algorithm is "order n", denoted by $O(n)$. Similarly, a quadratic-time algorithm is "order n squared", denoted by $O(n^2)$.

B.4 Summations

We have carried out summations multiple times in this book while analyzing algorithm complexities. So, let's look at a few summations, here, as an exercise.

- The sum of the first n positive integers can be calculated with the formula: $1 + 2 + 3 + 4 + ... + n = \frac{n(n+1)}{2}$. Example: $1 + 2 + 3 + 4 + 5 = \frac{5(5+1)}{2} = 16$.
- The sum of a finite geometric series is calculated with the formula: $a + ar + ar^2 + ... + ar^{n-1} = \frac{a(1-r^n)}{1-r}$, provided $r \neq 1$. Example:
$$5 + 5(3) + 5(3^2) + 5(3^3) = \frac{5(1-3^4)}{1-3}$$
$$\Rightarrow 5 + 15 + 45 + 135 = \frac{5(-80)}{-2}$$
$$\Rightarrow 200 = 200$$
- The sum of the squares of the first n integers can be calculated with the formula: $1^2 + 2^2 + 3^2 + 4^2 + ... + n^2 = \frac{n(n+1)(2n+1)}{6}$. Example: $1^2 + 2^2 + 3^2 + 4^2 = \frac{4(4+1)(8+1)}{6}$
$$\Rightarrow 1 + 4 + 9 + 16 = \frac{20(9)}{6}$$
$$\Rightarrow 30 = 30$$

B.5 Fibonacci Sequence

If you did your undergraduate degree in computer science, mathematics, or equivalent then you may have come across the *Fibonacci sequence* numerous times. Equation B.1 defines the *Fibonacci sequence*.

$$F_n = \begin{cases} 0, & \text{if } n = 0. \\ 1, & \text{if } n = 1. \\ F_{n-1} + F_{n-2} & \text{if } n > 1. \end{cases} \tag{B.1}$$

The first 11 numbers from the *Fibonacci sequence* can be seen in Table B.2.

Table B.2: Fibonacci numbers

n	0	1	2	3	4	5	6	7	8	9	10
F_n	0	1	1	2	3	5	8	13	21	34	55

B.6 Counting

Counting is a very useful technique in computing. Often we need to combine products from different categories to form new products. Health care and finance have many combinations and permutations of products and features. At a fundamental level, permutations and combinations can be applied in many fields. A resource orchestrator in Amazon's cloud can utilize combinatorial analysis for resource management and optimum allocation.

We have two basic counting principles—the sum rule principle and the product rule principle. Let's see their definitions and a few examples to realize those definitions.

- *Sum Rule Principle*: Suppose an event P can occur in m different ways and a second event Q can occur in n different ways, and they are mutually exclusive. Then P or Q can occur in $m + n$ different ways. Let's take an example to realize this definition. *Problem*: A computer science department has 10 different programming courses, 4 different mathematics courses, and 3 different management courses. How many ways can a student choose just one of the courses? *Solution*: The number of ways a student can choose just one of the courses = $n = (10 + 4 + 3) = 17$.
- *Product Rule Principle*: Suppose there are two independent events P and Q, which can occur in m and n different ways, respectively. Then the combination of P and Q can occur in mn different ways. Now, let's take an example to realize this definition. For the same problem described above, how many ways can a student choose one of each kind of course? *Solution*: The number of ways a student can choose one of each kind of course = $m = (10(4)(3)) = 120$.
- *Permutations*: This is a technique in which a set of n objects are arranged in a given order. We can take all the objects at a time or a subset of the objects. In terms of notation, the number of permutations of n objects taken r at a time is denoted by $P(n, r)$, $_nP_r$, or $P_{n,r}$. We can use a formula to calculate the number of permutations: $P(n, r) = n(n-1)(n-2)...(n-r+1) = \frac{n!}{(n-r)!}$. Example: let's say we have a set of five letters A, B, C, D, and E. How many permutations can be there if 3 of them are taken at a time? *Solution*: $n = 5$, $r = 3$. So $P(5, 3) = \frac{5!}{(5-3)!} = \frac{5(4)(3)(2)(1)}{2(1)} = 60$. So there can be 60 different permutations. Some valid permutations are $(ABC, ACB, BAC, BCA, CAB, CBA, BCD, BDC, CBD, CDB, DBC, DCB)$.
- *Combinations*: A combination of n elements, from a set having n elements, taken r at a time is any selection of r of the elements without considering the order. It

is denoted by $C(n,r)$, $_nC_r$, $C_{n,r}$, or C_r^n. A combination can be calculated using the
formula: $C(n,r) = \frac{P(n,r)}{r!} = \frac{n!}{r!(n-r)!}$. Sometimes, the following notation is used.

$$C(n,r) = \binom{n}{r}$$

Now let's solve the same problem that we used for permutation. The modified
problem is: we have a set of five letters A, B, C, D, and E. How many combina-
tions can be there if 3 of them are taken at a time? *Solution*: $C(5,3) = \frac{5!}{3!(5-3!)} = \frac{5(4)(3)(2)(1)}{(3)(2)(1)(2)(1)} = 10$. So there can be 10 different combinations.
Let's take one more example for combination.

Problem: A student buys 2 computer science books, 2 mathematics books, and
4 management books from a book store that has 4 computer science books, 5
mathematics books, and 8 management books. Find the number m of choices
that the student has.

Solution: The student can choose the computer science books in $C(4,2)$ ways,
the mathematics books in $C(5,2)$ ways, and the management books in $C(8,4)$
ways. Thus the number m of choices is:

$$
\begin{aligned}
m &= \binom{4}{2}\binom{5}{2}\binom{8}{4} = \frac{4!}{2!(2!)} \cdot \frac{5!}{2!(3!)} \cdot \frac{8!}{4!(4!)} \\
&= \frac{4\cdot3\cdot2\cdot1}{(2\cdot1)(2\cdot1)} \cdot \frac{5\cdot4\cdot3\cdot2\cdot1}{(2\cdot1)(3\cdot2\cdot1)} \cdot \frac{8\cdot7\cdot6\cdot5\cdot4\cdot3\cdot2\cdot1}{(4\cdot3\cdot2\cdot1)(4\cdot3\cdot2\cdot1)} \\
&= \frac{4\cdot3}{2\cdot1} \cdot \frac{5\cdot4}{2\cdot1} \cdot \frac{8\cdot7\cdot6\cdot5}{4\cdot3\cdot2\cdot1} \\
&= 6\cdot10\cdot70 = 4200
\end{aligned}
$$

So, the student has 4200 different choices. This should be interesting. The number of books that the store has, in each category, is less than 10, i.e., 4 in computer
science, 5 in mathematics, and 8 in management. The total number of books the
store has is 17. But the student has 4200 combinations available. Isn't that amaz-
ing? Now, we can think of Amazon Web Services. If there are 17 resources available currently, the AWS orchestrator could create thousands of combinations out
of those resources and present the combinations to customers.

Glossary

binary search tree A binary tree in which the value at the root node is greater than or equal to all the values in the left subtree and less than or equal to all the values in the right subtree.

breadth-first graph traversal In breadth-first traversal, a node's siblings are visited before its children.

degree of a tree The degree of a tree denotes how many children each node can have. The degree of a binary tree is 2.

depth of a node The length of its root path.

digraphs Directed graphs are called digraphs.

depth-first graph traversal In depth-first traversal, a node's children are visited before its siblings.

edge An edge connects two graph vertices.

height of a tree The greatest depth among all of the tree's nodes.

inorder tree traversal The left subtree is visited first, then the node, and finally the right subtree.

lazy evaluation Evaluation of expressions is done when the corresponding values are needed.

level in a tree The set of all nodes at a given depth.

memoization A technique in which calculations performed at previous steps are reused for efficiency.

path in a tree A sequence of nodes $(x_0, x_1, x_2, ..., x_n)$, where nodes with adjacent subscripts are adjacent nodes. Since trees are acyclic, a path cannot contain the same node more than once.

path length of a tree The sum of the lengths of all paths from its root.

© Springer Nature Switzerland AG 2019
B. P. Upadhyaya, *Data Structures and Algorithms with Scala*, Undergraduate
Topics in Computer Science, https://doi.org/10.1007/978-3-030-12561-5

preorder tree traversal The node is visited first, then the left subtree, and finally the right subtree.

postorder tree traversal The left subtree is visited first, then the right subtree, and finally the node.

root path For a node x_0, its root path is defined as a path $(x_0, x_1, x_2, ..., x_n)$, where x_n is the root of a tree.

size of a tree The number of non-leaf nodes in a tree.

vertex A graph node is called a vertex.

References

CMMK⁺18. P. Cudre-Mauroux, S. Madden, H. Kimura, M. Stonebraker, K. Lim, S. B. Zdonik, and J. Rogers. SS-DB: A Standard Science DBMS Benchmark. `http://people.csail.mit.edu/pcm/SSDB.pdf`, [Accessed 2018].

Col18. Scala Collections Performance Characteristics. `https://docs.scala-lang.org/overviews/collections/performance-characteristics.html`, [Accessed 2018].

DMB16. A. M. Dumitru, V. Merticariu, and P. Baumann. Array Database Scalability: Intercontinental Queries on Petabytes Datasets. In *Proceedings of the 28th International Conference on Scientific and Statistical Database Management*, 2016.

Lis18. Scala List. `https://github.com/scala/scala/blob/2.13.x/src/library/scala/collection/immutable/List.scala`, [Accessed 2018].

McC60. John McCarthy. Recursive Functions of Symbolic Expressions and Their Computation by Machine, Part I. *Communications of the ACM*, 3(4):184–195, April 1960.

Neo18. Neo4j. `https://neo4j.com/`, [Accessed 2018].

Sci18. SciDB. `https://www.paradigm4.com/`, [Accessed 2018].

SCMMS18. A. Seering, P. Cudre-Mauroux, S. Madden, and M. Stonebraker. Efficient Versioning for Scientific Array Databases. `http://db.csail.mit.edu/pubs/ArrayVersioning.pdf`, [Accessed 2018].

SS18. S. Sarawagi and M. Stonebraker. Efficient Organization of Large Multidimensional Arrays. `https://cs.brown.edu/courses/cs227/archives/2008/Papers/FileSystems/sarawagi94efficient.pdf`, [Accessed 2018].

Sto18. Michael Stonebraker. Big Data Means at Least Three Different Things... `https://www.nist.gov/sites/default/files/documents/itl/ssd/is/NIST-stonebraker.pdf`, [Accessed 2018].

© Springer Nature Switzerland AG 2019

B. P. Upadhyaya, *Data Structures and Algorithms with Scala*, Undergraduate Topics in Computer Science, https://doi.org/10.1007/978-3-030-12561-5

Index

© Springer Nature Switzerland AG 2019
B. P. Upadhyaya, *Data Structures and Algorithms with Scala*, Undergraduate
Topics in Computer Science, https://doi.org/10.1007/978-3-030-12561-5

Printed in the United States
By Bookmasters